YOUR INVITATION
COME AS YOU ARE

Lee Humphrey

WESTBOW
PRESS®
A DIVISION OF THOMAS NELSON
& ZONDERVAN

WestBow Press books may be ordered through booksellers or by contacting:

WestBow Press
A Division of Thomas Nelson & Zondervan
1663 Liberty Drive
Bloomington, IN 47403
www.westbowpress.com
1 (866) 928-1240

ISBN: 978-1-9736-1878-2 (sc)
ISBN: 978-1-9736-1880-5 (hc)
ISBN: 978-1-9736-1879-9 (e)

Library of Congress Control Number: 2018902209

Print information available on the last page.

WestBow Press rev. date: 5/24/2018

The thief cometh not, but for to steal, and to kill, and to destroy: I am come that they might have life, and that they might have it more abundantly.

John 10:10 (KJV)

DAY 1

In a world filled with deception, cruelty, abuse, and chaos, it's not hard to become paralyzed by fear and sink into hopelessness.

This book is to tell you there is a way out of that prison.

When everyone has turned their backs on you and said, "You're hopeless," there is a friend who will put His arm around you and walk you out to freedom.

These pages will introduce you to Him. Please read only one page each day. Read it over again and let it become truth to you. Only then will you be ready for the next day's writing.

Several different translations of the Bible have been used in these pages. When you see the designation *KJV*, that scripture is from the King James Version. Do you have a problem with all those *thees* and *thous*? Go to the last two pages in this book for a few tips to make it easier to read that version.

This author has a heart for those who are hurting and was led to write this just for you. May you be freed from your hopelessness and fear and begin to look forward to a life filled with joy and expectation.

This book did not come into your hands by accident. Now turn the page and begin your new life. See for yourself why you are special.

Day 2

My friend, who has a jail ministry, shared some letters from the incarcerated women, and there was a recurring theme in them all—fear. Fear of failure, fear of being alone or forgotten, fear of what the future might hold, fear that their families and friends would forget them, fear of falling back into sin. My heart ached for them. But all those same fears can be real to anyone—inside a prison or walking free on the streets. Wherever we live, fear is the real prison that keeps us bound. That's why 1 John 4:18 (KJV) is where we start:

> There is no fear in love; but perfect love casteth out fear: because fear hath torment. He that feareth is not made perfect in love.

How are we made perfect in love? By inviting the perfect one into our hearts and surrendering our entire being to Him. There's a simple way that leads to doing just that. It's a term I heard long ago; it's *the Roman Road*. Let's take a walk.

DAY 3

Romans 3:23 (KJV) informs us, "For all have sinned, and come short of the glory of God."

You're not alone—notice the word *all*. All have sinned—that's you, me, and everyone in the world. But God, in His mercy, gave us a way out of living in sin. It's in Romans 6:23 (KJV):

> For the wages of sin is death; but the gift of God is eternal
> life through Jesus Christ our Lord.

What a gift! Eternal life—something to look forward to when we leave this earth and the hope we need to face a world full of fear.

Every year at the Christmas season, we celebrate that gift from God. On that long-ago night of His birth, there was fear in the dark fields, but even then God soothed them with these words we can read in Luke 2:10 (KJV):

> And the angel said unto them, Fear not: for behold, I bring
> you good tidings of great joy, which shall be to all people.

Notice again that you're not alone—it's great joy for all!

Continuing down the Roman Road, we find conviction in Romans 10:9–10 (KJV).

> That if thou shalt confess with thy mouth the Lord Jesus, and shalt believe in thine heart that God hath raised Him from the dead, thou shalt be saved. For with the heart man believeth unto righteousness; and with the mouth confession is made unto salvation.

Jesus, God's only son, came to earth for you and me. He voluntarily gave His life that we might have that salvation leading to eternal life.

Even though this scripture originally spoken by Jesus doesn't specifically mention fear, it will soothe yours. Read Matthew 11:28 (KJV):

> Come unto me, all ye that labour and are heavy laden, and I will give you rest.

Peace I leave with you; my peace I give you. I do not give to you as the world gives. Do not let your hearts be troubled and do not be afraid.

John 14:27 (NIV)

Day 5

After Jesus died on the cross, he was buried in a sealed tomb. In Matthew's account, some women went to the tomb at dawn. Imagine their feelings when they saw an angel sitting on the stone in front of it! He must have been a big, powerful, angel because he frightened them in the early morning hours before the sun rose. But what were his words?

> And the angel answered and said unto the women, Fear not ye: for I know that ye seek Jesus, which was crucified. He is not here: for he is risen, as he said. Come, see the place where the Lord lay. (Matthew 28:5–6 KJV)

Naturally the women ran away to tell Jesus's followers this wonderful news, and who should they meet on the road? Jesus! Read His words in Matthew 28:10a (KJV:

> Then said Jesus unto them, Be not afraid.

The one who fears is not made perfect in love. Let's turn that into *the one who does not fear is made perfect in love.*

DAY 6

Does that mean if I fear, I'm not made perfect in love?

Absolutely not! This fear is the fear of God's judgment day. When we realize how much God loves us, that fear is driven out. Thanks to Jesus and His death on the cross for us, God sees us as if we had never done anything wrong. Have you arrived at the point of realization of God's love for you? If not, you're in a crowd. The first step in this process is to forgive yourself. Read Psalm 103:6 and 103:8–12 (MSG).

> God makes everything come out right; He puts victims back on their feet. God is sheer mercy and grace; not easily angered, he's rich in love. He doesn't endlessly nag and scold, nor hold grudges forever. He doesn't treat us as our sins deserve, nor pay us back in full for our wrongs. As high as heaven is over the earth, so strong is his love to those who fear him. And as far as sunrise is from sunset, he has separated us from our sins.

If the God of the universe feels this way about our pasts, can't we accept His love and forgive ourselves?

DAY 7

"So strong is His love for those who fear Him," wrote the psalmist.

What's this? I'm trying to get free from fear, and here's the Bible telling me I must fear God to be loved by Him!

Yes, there are some good fears in the Bible. A child is taught not to play in the street because there is a fear of being hit by a truck. But does that mean he's so afraid of trucks that he won't ride in one? Of course not. He has a respect for the power of that truck as it comes down the road. That's a very loose interpretation of the fear of God—it's respect, reverence, and realization that He is a holy God. Another good fear is found in Matthew 10:28–31 (MSG).

> Don't be bluffed into silence by the threats of bullies. There's nothing they can do to your soul, your core being. Save your fear for God, who holds your entire life—body and soul—in His hands. What's the price of a pet canary? Some loose change, right? And God cares what happens to it even more than you do. He pays even greater attention to you, down to the last detail—even numbering the hairs on your head! So don't be intimidated by all this bully talk. You're worth more than a million canaries.

DAY 8

Now that we have this difference between bad fear and good fear straightened out, let's look at some of the ways you are truly loved. We could finish out this entire book in scriptures about the many ways that God loves us, but read this one.

> Do you think anyone is going to be able to drive a wedge between us and Christ's love for us? There is no way! Not trouble, not hard times, not hatred, not hunger, not homelessness, not bullying threats, not backstabbing, not even the worst sins listed in Scripture. (Romans 8:35 MSG)

And then the message continues in Romans.

> I'm absolutely convinced that nothing—nothing living or dead, angelic or demonic, today or tomorrow, high or low, thinkable or unthinkable—absolutely nothing can get between us and God's love because of the way that Jesus our Master has embraced us. (Romans 8:38–39 MSG)

This verse casts a different light on the meaning of the fear of God, doesn't it? When someone loves us that much, how can we not be in reverent awe toward Him?

DAY 9

Now we know that God loves us and forgives us, but are you having an issue with forgiving and loving yourself? Take heart! You are not alone. That's why there's an answer in the Bible. God, in his infinite wisdom, knew that would happen. Let's look at Proverbs 19:8 (AMP):

> He who gains wisdom *and* good sense loves (preserves) his own soul; He who keeps understanding will find good *and* prosper.

According to this scripture, it's wise to love yourself—and to also preserve your own soul. *Preserve* means *protect and maintain. Soul* means *a breathing creature.* Are you a breathing creature? If so, when you gain wisdom and good sense, you love yourself!

I admit there are times when I don't even like myself—much less love myself! At those times, I need more wisdom, don't I? Where do we get wisdom? There's a scripture for that—Proverbs 1:7 (MSG):

> Start with God—the first step in learning is bowing down to God; only fools thumb their noses at such wisdom and learning.

Well, that's clear now, isn't it? And where do we find God's wisdom? In His Word—the Bible.

DAY 10

There was a time in my life when I was so down, so fearful, so depressed that I couldn't see a way out. A wise friend suggested, with all the love she had, that I read Proverbs. Because I had no other answers, I thought I would try it. I read it slowly and reread some verses often. It's a book so filled with God's wisdom that, no matter how many times you read it, you will find something new every time. Here's a sample from Proverbs 1:1–6 (TLB).

> These are the proverbs of King Solomon of Israel, David's son: He wrote them to teach his people how to live—how to act in every circumstance, for he wanted them to be understanding, just, and fair in everything they did. "I want to make the simpleminded wise!" he said. "I want to warn young men about some problems they will face. I want those already wise to become wiser and become leaders by exploring the depths of meaning in these nuggets of truth."

Dear friend, listen well to my words;
tune your ears to my voice.
Keep my message in plain view at all times.
Concentrate! Learn it by heart!
Those who discover these words live, really live;
body and soul, they're bursting with health.
Proverbs 4:20-22 (MSG)

Day 11

I knew my friend meant her advice for my good, but I needed something specific—you know, a booming voice from heaven. But when I read that last sentence, the word *truth* stood out as if it had a spotlight on it. How could I find the truth that would give me an answer for my specific situation? You guessed it! There's a verse for that. Read it in John 8:31–32 (KJV).

> Then said Jesus to those Jews which believed on him, If ye continue in my word, then are ye my disciples indeed; And ye shall know the truth, and the truth shall make you free.

There's that word *truth* again. And it's what will set me free? Free from what? Free—period! Free from all those fears? You bet it will, and staying in that truth will free you from tomorrow's fears. Was this my invitation to start reading all the books on truth? Not quite—just the one that God wrote, God's book. Read Titus 1:2 (VOICE).

> We rest in this hope we've been given—the hope that we will live forever with our God—the hope that He proclaimed ages and ages ago (even before time began). And our God is no liar; He is not even capable of uttering lies.

Day 12

God is no liar. I can certainly accept that. But what about all those people He used to write all the books of the Bible? For the answer I searched the source of all truth and found it in 2 Timothy 3:16–17 (TLB).

> The whole Bible was given to us by inspiration from God and is useful to teach us what is true and to make us realize what is wrong in our lives; it straightens us out and helps us do what is right. It is God's way of making us well prepared at every point, fully equipped to do good to everyone.

Let's now move fast-forward from that low time to when I felt God telling me to write a book. After all my excuses and efforts to get out of it because I wasn't capable of doing the job, He planted a vision in my head. It was a giant hand, holding a pencil. I was the pencil! A pencil can do nothing without a hand to direct what it writes. That's exactly how He used all those great people—as "pencils" to record His words in the Bible. And what a lesson to me! I'm not able to write a book—not without Him.

Day 13

Back in my younger years, I often dreamed of what I would become—I had visions of grandeur. As I grew a little older and wiser, I had fewer visions of grandeur and more apprehension. What did my future hold? Have you ever had a fear about your future—not the distant future but next week, next month, or next year? I believe we've all been there—or are there. Back to the real truth for some comfort in Jeremiah 29:11 (TLB):

> For I know the plans I have for you, says the Lord. They are plans for good and not for evil, to give you a future and a hope.

Wow! God has a plan for my life? It's a good plan, and it will give me a future and a hope. There's that word *hope* again. Can we just hope for anything, or are we fooling ourselves? Let's dig into *hope*. We find it again in Hebrews 11:1 (KJV):

> Now faith is the substance of things hoped for, the evidence of things not seen.

Day 14

Do I need both faith and hope? It would seem that's correct. As humans, we pretty well have the hope concept down. Faith? That's another story. Again, there's an answer for that in the Bible—in Romans 10:17 (NIV):

> Consequently, faith comes from hearing the message, and the message is heard through the word about Christ.

We've made a circle back to the Bible—that's where we get faith—by the Word. Sound familiar? That's because it was the scripture used just a few days ago, and it is so important that it bears repeating.

> The whole Bible was given to us by inspiration from God and is useful to teach us what is true and to make us realize what is wrong in our lives; it straightens us out and helps us do what is right. It is God's way of making us well prepared at every point, fully equipped to do good to everyone. (2 Timothy 3:16–17 TLB)

Daily Bible reading is as essential to your spiritual health as daily eating is essential to your physical health. But you also need to chew your food in order for it not to choke you. The same is true for God's Word. Read a verse and then "chew" on it—don't let it choke you up if you don't understand what it means. Ask God to give you the meaning; ask your trusted Christian friend or pastor. Put it on your memory shelf to revisit and continue reading and chewing.

DAY 15

Just how important is faith? Let's see what God has to say to that question.

> But without faith it is impossible to please him: for he
> that cometh to God must believe that he is, and that he
> is a rewarder of them that diligently seek him. (Hebrews
> 11:6 KJV)

Oh, my—that puts the importance of faith in a different light, doesn't it?
I did a little study on the meaning of *to seek* and went back to Greek, the
language used in the New Testament. It means *to search out, investigate,
crave*. That seems to me that we should search the Bible for what God says to
us, investigate what His Word says about how we should live, and crave the
living, breathing God of the universe every minute of every day. I wonder if
God means that if we start searching in His Word, it will give us curiosity to
investigate further, and we will then crave a closer relationship with Him.
It's kind of hard to crave something you've never tasted, isn't it?

Day 16

But what if I've lost all hope? I can't see a way out of this mess. Does the Bible really have anything for me? Yes! Yes! Yes!

> Hear my prayer, O Lord, give ear to my supplications: in thy faithfulness answer me, and in thy righteousness. And enter not into judgment with thy servant; for in thy sight shall no man living be justified. For the enemy hath persecuted my soul; he hath smitten my life down to the ground; he hath made me to dwell in darkness, as those that have been long dead. Therefore is my spirit overwhelmed within me; my heart within me is desolate. I remember the days of old; I meditate on all thy works; I muse on the work of thy hands. I stretch forth my hands unto thee; my soul thirsteth after thee, as a thirsty land. (Psalm 143:1–6 KJV)

God understands your feelings. He knows your situation. Cling to Him and don't give up. Tomorrow brings back hope.

DAY 17

Hopelessness is not godlessness. He's always there, always present. He is the great *I AM*.

> Hear me speedily, O Lord: my spirit faileth; hide not thy face from me, lest I be like unto them that go down into the pit. Cause me to hear thy lovingkindness in the morning; for in thee do I trust; cause me to know the way wherein I should walk; for I lift up my soul unto thee. Deliver me, O Lord, from mine enemies: I flee unto thee to hide me. Teach me to do thy will; for thou art my God: thy spirit is good; lead me into the land of uprightness. Quicken me, O Lord, for thy name's sake: for thy righteousness' sake bring my soul out of trouble. And of thy mercy cut off mine enemies, and destroy all them that afflict my soul: for I am thy servant. (Psalm 143:7–12 KJV)

It's okay to pour out your heart to God. He is there, just waiting for you to ask for His help. Give Him a chance to change your life.

Day 18

Have you ever wished God would just hurry up and answer your prayer? You are not alone! I've wanted to tell Him to come on and catch up with me because I've got this situation all figured out, if He would just provide the way. But over the years, I've found that God's timing is perfect—every time—even when I wished it wasn't. I've also learned that the wait was good for me! See why in Isaiah 40:31 (KJV).

> But they that wait upon the Lord shall renew their strength;
> they shall mount up with wings as eagles; they shall run,
> and not be weary; they shall walk, and not faint.

Taking the time to chew on this verse will reveal several meanings. For me, the strength that was renewed was spiritual. While waiting, I sought God with all my heart, studied His Word, and started a new habit of beginning each day with prayer. When the thing I had been waiting for arrived, I found the scriptures I had studied were just what I needed. Without that preparation, I would have failed. My job became a labor of love that I could run with, and I did not grow weary of doing it. When I needed to slow down and walk, I didn't lose faith. You see, waiting was just what I needed!

Day 19

I've heard others talk about waiting on the Lord in terms of days or weeks or months. Not for us! My spouse and I waited ten years for the first big journey we felt God calling us to undertake! Did we give up at times? Yes. Did we doubt that we had really heard God? Yes. Did we try to make it happen on our own? Yes—and that was costly. But we kept coming back to the original calling every time. We kept holding onto several scriptures, Isaiah 40:31 and this one in Esther. The queen was facing a tough life-and-death decision. Read the advice she received in Esther 4:14b (KJV):

> And who knoweth whether thou art come to the kingdom
> for such a time as this?

Isn't it worth the wait to be in that perfect place that God has planned for you? And once you learn how to wait, does that mean you won't ever have to do it again? No! In fact, we are in the midst of another wait, and it's already been four years. But God's timing is always perfect, and we are content to wait on Him.

Day 20

Have you ever wondered about the purpose of waiting—except the obvious one—to get us ready? Perhaps it's because we don't count time the way God does. Read 2 Peter 3:8 (KJV):

> But, beloved, be not ignorant of this one thing, that one day is with the Lord as a thousand years, and a thousand years as one day.

I don't believe the human mind can grasp eternity. Everything around us has a beginning and an ending. A seed is planted; it sprouts, produces flowers, and dies. Our pets are born, live their lives, and then they die. We do the same. But to God, who has always existed and always will, our days are a drop in the bucket. The lifespan of a housefly is twenty-eight days compared to our lifespan of nearly 29,000 days. There's no way to compare our days to eternity because it never ends. Instead, we should heed God in Psalm 37:7–9 (KJV).

> Rest in the Lord, and wait patiently for him: fret not thyself because of him who prospereth in his way, because of the man who bringeth wicked devices to pass. Cease from anger, and forsake wrath: fret not thyself in any wise to do evil. For evildoers shall be cut off: but those that wait upon the Lord, they shall inherit the earth.

Easier said than done, right? This is a huge step. Don't get upset, show no anger or rage, and don't worry? What does God have in mind?

DAY 21

Worry, by definition, is giving way to anxiety or unease or allowing one's mind to dwell on difficulty or troubles. So worry is fear—usually of something that might happen but over which you have no control. Do you worry about your future? Do you worry about your family and their futures? Are you dreading what tomorrow or the next day might bring?

Read Jesus's words in John 16:33 (KJV):

> These things I have spoken unto you, that in me ye might have peace. In the world ye shall have tribulation: but be of good cheer; I have overcome the world.

It seems that Jesus knew what we would face, doesn't it? Here's one solution from Psalm 55:22 (KJV):

> Cast thy burden upon the Lord, and he shall sustain thee: he shall never suffer the righteous to be moved.

Here's where getting to know the Word comes in. He will never let (suffer) the righteous be shaken (moved). Are you righteous? We will look at that tomorrow.

DAY 22

What exactly does it mean to be righteous? The dictionary defines the word as "acting in accord with divine or moral law: free from guilt or sin." Wow! That lets me out—how about you? But what does the Bible tell us? Here's Romans 3:10 (KJV):

> As it is written, There is none righteous, no, not one.

Now that's a downer. If no one is righteous, then what hope is there? Is the Bible written just for truly holy people and not for me? No! Here's what God says about that.

> But now God has shown us a different way to heaven—not by "being good enough" and trying to keep his laws, but by a new way (though not new, really, for the Scriptures told about it long ago). Now God says he will accept and acquit us—declare us "not guilty"—if we trust Jesus Christ to take away our sins. And we all can be saved in this same way, by coming to Christ, no matter who we are or what we have been like. (Romans 3:21–22 TLB)

Now I understand why they call the Bible the good news!

DAY 23

Okay, now I understand—once I accepted Jesus into my heart and asked Him to forgive me, I was freed, and my past was forgotten by Him. But what about now? I did something stupid just this morning! Am I already unsaved? Am I the only one with this problem? Not according to God's word. Read Romans 7:15–17 (TLB).

> I don't understand myself at all, for I really want to do what is right, but I can't. I do what I don't want to—what I hate. I know perfectly well that what I am doing is wrong, and my bad conscience proves that I agree with these laws I am breaking. But I can't help myself because I'm no longer doing it. It is sin inside me that is stronger than I am that makes me do these evil things.

What? I thought I got rid of all that sin when I accepted Jesus. Do I still have to repent (turn away) from sin every day? It looks that way. Man, do I really need some help here. What's the answer, God? Read on.

Day 24

Will I ever arrive at this new life as a Christian? Well, if you do, please tell the world, because you will be the first person in history! You've heard of a life-changing experience? Following Jesus is a life of changing experiences. He works on us every day—thank goodness! I need that. Want some more of that good news? Focus on Romans 8:1–4 (TLB).

> So there is now no condemnation awaiting those who belong to Christ Jesus. For the power of the life-giving Spirit—and this power is mine through Christ Jesus—has freed me from the vicious circle of sin and death. We aren't saved from sin's grasp by knowing the commandments of God because we can't and don't keep them, but God put into effect a different plan to save us. He sent his own Son in a human body like ours—except that ours are sinful— and destroyed sin's control over us by giving himself as a sacrifice for our sins. So now we can obey God's laws if we follow after the Holy Spirit and no longer obey the old evil nature within us.

The answer to obeying God's laws is after that big *if* in the last sentence. We must follow after the Holy Spirit. How does that work?

DAY 25

We are back to that concept of righteousness. Jesus gives us guidance for that in Matthew 5:6 (KJV):

> Blessed are they which do hunger and thirst after righteousness: for they shall be filled."

Filled? With what—fried chicken and iced tea? That wouldn't last very long. Jesus had something more in mind—something that will last a lifetime. It's this very same Jesus who promised eternal life and something else in John 14:15–16 (TLB).

> If you love me, obey me; and I will ask the Father and he will give you another Comforter, and he will never leave you. He is the Holy Spirit, the Spirit who leads into all truth. The world at large cannot receive him, for it isn't looking for him and doesn't recognize him. But you do, for he lives with you now and some day shall be in you.

Why not make that *some day* today? Jesus has already made this gift available to you. All it takes from you is an invitation to the Holy Spirit to take over your life and guide you on the path that leads to righteousness.

The invitation can be a simple, "Holy Spirit, I need you to come into my life and take control. I accept, by faith, that what Jesus promised In John 14, is now mine. I invite you to live in me and be my guide."

DAY 26

Now that you have asked the Holy Spirit to live in you and fill you with His presence, what will He do? What's His purpose? I'm glad you asked that!

Here is Jesus's answer just a few verses down in John 14:26 (AMP).

> But the Helper (Comforter, Advocate, Intercessor—Counselor, Strengthener, Standby), the Holy Spirit, whom the Father will send in My name (in My place to represent Me and act on My behalf), He will teach you all things. And He will help you remember everything that I have told you.

My goodness! I count seven titles for the Holy Spirit, but add two more—Teacher and Reminder. Each title represents promises that we are never alone. Can you imagine having all those professionals at your fingertips? Take heart—you don't have to imagine any longer—it's a reality! The Holy Spirit is living in you and just waiting for you to ask. Ask what? Anything.

DAY 27

Let's take some time to explore each of the Holy Spirit's names. We will start with *Helper*. One of the definitions of a helper is this: an extra locomotive attached to a train at the front, middle, or rear, especially to provide extra power for climbing a steep grade.

Have you ever faced a problem or situation that looked like a mountain to you? One that you didn't have the energy (or power) to climb? So did the apostle Paul when he had asked God to take away a problem. God answered him a different way in 2 Corinthians 12:9a (KJV):

> And he said unto me, My grace is sufficient for thee: for my strength is made perfect in weakness.

Let's see—the Holy Spirit was sent to us as a representative of Jesus, and He's now our Helper (power). Going all the way back to the Greek, we find that in this instance, *power* means *ability*. With that in mind, once you have invited the Holy Spirit to fill you completely, you have at your disposal that power to conquer the steep hill you are facing. You are not alone!

DAY 28

Next on our list of names for the Holy Spirit is *Comforter*. This isn't a bed covering; however, a bed comforter can certainly keep you warm on a cold winter's night. No, this is a living comforter—one who wraps His arms around you in the middle of trouble and makes you feel that everything will turn out for good. That warm, fuzzy feeling—peace.

It's what Jesus promised us in John 14:27 (KJV):

> Peace I leave with you, my peace I give unto you: not as the world giveth, give I unto you. Let not your heart be troubled, neither let it be afraid.

What greater peace is there than freedom from fear? Here is peace, and the comforter who gives it lives within you!

Do you have a tough decision looming ahead of you? Weigh your choices and ask the Holy Spirit to give you peace with the one that is best for your future. Should you do so even if all your choices are good ones, but you still need to pick just one? That's right. Go with the one that gives you peace.

Trust the Holy Spirit as your comforter when fear comes into your life. Let Him guide you. He wants only the best for you.

Day 29

The two words *advocate* and *intercessor,* describing the Holy Spirit, seem to go together. An advocate is one who pleads the cause of or in favor of another. The Bible says we have an advocate in heaven. It's found in 1 John 2:1 (KJV):

> My little children, these things write I unto you, that ye sin not. And if any man sin, we have an advocate with the Father, Jesus Christ the righteous.

Remember that before Jesus went back to heaven, he promised the gift of the Holy Spirit to represent him here on earth? So He, the Holy Spirit, is our advocate here, and He intercedes on our behalf with Jesus, who sits at the right hand of the heavenly Father.

Day 30

But what about those times when we just don't know how to pray? Those tough times when we really want to pray, but just can't find the words? That's where the Holy Spirit, our intercessor, comes to the rescue. That promise is in Romans 8:26 (TLB).

> And in the same way—by our faith—the Holy Spirit helps us with our daily problems and in our praying. For we don't even know what we should pray for nor how to pray as we should, but the Holy Spirit prays for us with such feeling that it cannot be expressed in words.

What a blessed gift! But wait—there's more.

DAY 31

Moving on with this incredible list of just who the Holy Spirit is to us, we find that he is our counselor. A counselor is a person trained to give guidance on personal, social, or psychological problems. Remember when we talked about following after the Holy Spirit? Here's another reason to do just that.

Are you facing a decision and don't know which way to turn? And there's no human counselor at your door? Your friend, in whom you always confide, is out of town? Sometimes we look for answers everywhere—except where the true answers are always available. You have the best counselor in the universe living right inside you! Ask the Holy Spirit. Read the passage in which Jesus was preparing His disciples for the time when He would no longer be on earth for them to ask their questions. He wanted them to understand they would not be alone.

> But when the Friend comes, the Spirit of the Truth, he will take you by the hand and guide you into all the truth there is. He won't draw attention to himself, but will make sense out of what is about to happen and, indeed out of all that I have done and said. He will honor me, he will take from me and deliver it to you. Everything the Father has is also mine. That is why I've said, 'He takes from me and delivers to you.' (John 16:13–15 MSG)

You do have a direct line to heaven!

DAY 32

Now we come to the last two names given to the Holy Spirit: strengthener and standby.

Standby means "one to be relied on, especially in emergencies" and "a favorite or reliable choice or resource." Since the Holy Spirit never sleeps, I love the definition of "on standby"—ready or available for immediate action or use. This means you have a helper, a comforter, an advocate, an intercessor, and a counselor—all ready and available for immediate action or use!

The final name is *strengthener*. Almost all gyms have a strength trainer who uses machines to help clients build muscular strength. The Holy Spirit has the word of truth to help you build spiritual strength for living in today's world. But the strength trainer can only point the way to those machines to help you; it's you who must use the machine. So it is with the word of truth—it's you who has to open it up and allow the Holy Spirit to teach you from it and thus gain that spiritual strength.

> The whole Bible was given to us by inspiration from God and is useful to teach us what is true and to make us realize what is wrong in our lives; it straightens us out and helps us do what is right. It is God's way of making us well prepared at every point, fully equipped to do good to everyone. (2 Timothy 3:16–17 TLB)

Enough said.

Day 33

Are you ready to be strengthened through the Word of God? Just as in a gym, when you take off those clothes you wore to dress in preparation for training, let's look at what needs to be removed first.

Paul tells us in Hebrews 12:15 (NASB):

> See to it that no one comes short of the grace of God; that no root of bitterness springing up causes trouble, and by it many be defiled.

Part of the *Urban Dictionary*'s definition of *bitterness* is "a feeling of deep anger and resentment." Bitterness is an emotion that encompasses both anger and hate. Bitterness is often the result of some past event that has hurt, scarred, and jaded the person.

Notice the Bible mentions a root of bitterness—not a seed. A root begins as a seed and takes time to grow into a root. Sometimes a past event has hurt us so deeply that it stays with us for a lifetime—a seed that has had plenty of time to grow into a root.

Now we are told to get rid of that root—or we may miss out on God's grace. *Grace* is a small word with a big meaning that we will investigate later, but if you're like me, you don't want to miss out on anything that God offers you! So how do we get rid of that root of bitterness? Let's read on.

Day 34

A hurt not forgotten stays in our minds and emotions. That hurt becomes unforgiveness. Unforgiveness becomes bitterness toward the person who caused it. Bitterness toward a person grows from a seed to a root, and it clouds our judgment, makes us suspicious of others who might also hurt us, and blocks our ability to love someone truly. And suddenly there is that root of bitterness!

Now if we work backward from the root of bitterness, we find that hurt. Avoiding facing that hurt might seem to keep us from worse hurt, but it does just the opposite—it causes more hurt.

The Bible is very blunt about unforgiveness. Read Ephesians 4:32 (KJV):

> And be ye kind one to another, tenderhearted, forgiving one
> another, even as God for Christ's sake hath forgiven you.

Notice that nowhere in that scripture do we read, "whenever you feel like it or when that person apologizes to you or because they deserve it." It just directs us to forgive.

Forgiving has nothing to do with your feelings—it is a choice. You choose to forgive. But what about the culprits? They didn't apologize. Shouldn't they have to do something also? No. To forgive is up to you. It won't change that person. It won't rewrite the past and make everything okay. So why should I forgive?

DAY 35

Why should I forgive? Let's look back at that last phrase in Ephesians 4:32 (KJV):

> even as God for Christ's sake hath forgiven you.

Jesus is God, who came to the earth in the flesh—as a human being. He chose to give himself as a sacrifice for your sins so that you could have eternal life. He's given you a free choice. You can choose to forgive or choose not to forgive. What happens if you choose not to forgive? Read what Jesus said in Matthew 6:14–15 (MSG).

> In prayer there is a connection between what God does and what you do. You can't get forgiveness from God, for instance, without also forgiving others. If you refuse to do your part, you cut yourself off from God's part.

That makes forgiving more than important, doesn't it? So what does it mean to forgive? The dictionary defines the verb *forgive* as "stop feeling angry or resentful toward (someone) for an offense, flaw, or mistake."

Jesus didn't say it would be easy. Someone I thought was a dear friend deeply hurt me. I knew I had to forgive her, but knowing and doing are different matters. So I forgave her. But the next time I saw her, all that hurt and resentment came back. Does that mean I didn't truly forgive her? Let's see what Jesus has to say about that in tomorrow's reading.

So, chosen by God for this new life of love, dress in the wardrobe God picked out for you: compassion, kindness, humility, quiet strength, discipline. Be even-tempered, content with second place, quick to forgive an offense. Forgive as quickly and completely as the Master forgave you. And regardless of what else you put on, wear love. It's your basic, all-purpose garment. Never be without it.
Colossians 3:12-14 (MSG)

Day 36

What if you truly forgive someone, but then that hurt comes back? Focus on this conversation between Peter and Jesus in Matthew 18:21–22 (MSG).

> At that point Peter got up the nerve to ask, "Master, how many times do I forgive a brother or sister who hurts me? Seven?" Jesus replied, "Seven! Hardly. Try seventy times seven."

In other words—forgive a culprit as many times as it takes! I didn't count, but I was probably close to that seventy times seven.

Did that make it right—what she had done? No, but it made me right with God.

The choice won't be an easy one. It's much easier to harbor resentment and feel you've been wronged, even if you did nothing to deserve it. Perhaps it goes back to your childhood, when you were truly the innocent one. But the choice is still yours. You may have to keep on forgiving until you get it sealed in your heart, but the benefits far outweigh the other choice.

Forgiving others is for *your* good—not those who hurt you. They may never know you forgave them—but the one who matters will know. Didn't we mention grace a while back? What about grace?

Day 37

A few days ago, we looked at Hebrews 12:15 (NASB), which cautions us not to miss out on God's grace. What is grace? The word occurs in the New Testament over a hundred times, so it must be important for us to know the meaning.

The traditional meaning in today's language is "the unmerited favor of God." Let's break that down a bit. *Unmerited* means *undeserved or not paid for*—a gift. *Favor,* in the original Greek, means "the divine influence upon the heart, and its reflection in the life (including gratitude)." Remember this is the favor *of God.* When your life is in favor with God, He gives you the strength to live a godly life.

Where is this unmerited favor we are told not to miss? You already have it! Read John 1:17 (AMP):

> For the Law was given through Moses, but grace (the unearned, undeserved favor of God) and truth came through Jesus Christ.

The good news is that when you accepted Jesus Christ as your Lord and Savior, you were (and are) given grace.

Now you might ask, "What do I do with this gift of grace?" Read on.

DAY 38

Peter wrote two letters that we know of to his Christian friends. In the last verse of the second letter, 2 Peter 3:18 (KJV), he summed up what was important for his friends:

> But grow in grace, and in the knowledge of our Lord and
> Savior Jesus Christ. To him be glory both now and for ever.
> Amen.

Now that I have this gift of grace, I'm supposed to grow in it. How do I do that? How do I make the gift of God's favor grow?

We do so by doing what is pleasing to Him. We get to know Him. How? The same way you get to know anyone. Spend time with Him. There are many ways, but the first I always think of is prayer—talking to God and listening to Him.

I've been a Christian for many years and thought I had a prayer life because, when I needed something, I asked God for it. I was always asking—for wisdom, for Him to bless my plans, to bless the food I was eating, to forgive me when I did wrong. You get the idea—God was my resource when I wanted or needed something. But one day that all changed.

Day 39

Suddenly my eyes were opened to what prayer really is—building a relationship with Him. How did God do that in my life? *How* doesn't really matter—*what* He showed me does. Your prayer life may be quite different from mine. The important issue is that you have a real prayer life.

One of my favorite Bible verses on prayer is 2 Chronicles 7:14 (KJV).

> If my people, which are called by my name, shall humble themselves, and pray, and seek my face, and turn from their wicked ways; then will I hear from heaven, and will forgive their sin, and will heal their land.

This is one of many promises that God will hear when you pray. Here's another, Proverbs 15:29 (KJV):

> The Lord is far from the wicked: but he heareth the prayer of the righteous.

Another is found in Colossians 4:2 (AMP):

> Be persistent and devoted to prayer, being alert and focused in your prayer life with an attitude of thanksgiving.

Here also is Jeremiah 29:12 (MSG):

> When you call on me, when you come and pray, I'll listen.

I could keep on, but I think you get the idea. God wants you to spend time with Him—talking, listening, and getting to know Him better.

Day 40

Here are a few practical tips on prayer that I have learned. Find a spot. It may be a comfortable chair or propped up in bed. Make it your prayer place and go there every day.

Write down your prayers and date them. This gives you a journal of prayers to revisit each day. Add more as you think of someone or something that needs God's attention. Date the day God answers your prayer. Nothing builds continuing faith like having a prayer answered.

What about those days when you just don't feel like praying? Go to your spot anyway and use ACTS.

Adoration—tell God how great He is, how wonderful He is, and give Him praise.

Confession—tell God about the goofs you've had and ask for His forgiveness.

Thanksgiving—thank God for everything—the air you breathe, the food you eat, all the benefits He has provided.

Supplication—make your requests. By the time you get to the *S*, you will be pumped and ready to spend time with the God of the universe!

The most important advice I can give is to be consistent and pray every day. I start each day in prayer because I found that if I didn't do it first, the business of the day took over, and suddenly it was evening, and I hadn't prayed. Don't have enough time in the morning? Get up earlier!

Day 41

Jesus spoke often about prayer, once in Matthew 6:7 (NIRV):

> When you pray, do not keep talking on and on. That is what
> ungodly people do. They think they will be heard because
> they talk a lot.

Our heavenly Father doesn't want you to pretend to be something you are not. He desires honesty and openness. So be yourself when you pray. It's okay to pray out loud or in silence. He has really good hearing!

This is a new way of life for you, I know. But perseverance does have its rewards. Do you feel weak, and do your prayers seem to be hitting the ceiling and bouncing back? God has an answer for that in 1 Chronicles 16:11 (KJV):

> Seek the Lord and his strength, seek His face continually.

Our God, who never sleeps, is always there, and He will give you the strength you need as you start this new walk. Believe me, it's worth continuing!

Day 42

Perhaps you are saying: "Okay, I prayed every day for a week, and nothing happened. I'm kind of tired of this. When does He start answering?" Read the words of Jesus in Luke 18:1–8a (AMP).

> Now Jesus was telling the disciples a parable to make the point that at all times they ought to pray and not give up and lose heart, saying, "In a certain city there was a judge who did not fear God and had no respect for man. There was a (desperate) widow in that city and she kept coming to him and saying, 'Give me justice and legal protection from my adversary.' For a time he would not; but later he said to himself, 'Even though I do not fear God nor respect man, yet because this widow continues to bother me, I will give her justice and legal protection; otherwise by continually coming she (will be an intolerable annoyance and she) will wear me out." Then the Lord said, "Listen to what the unjust judge says! And will not (our just) God defend and avenge His elect (His chosen ones) who cry out to Him day and night? Will He delay (in providing justice) on their behalf? I tell you that He will defend and avenge them quickly.

So how quick is quickly?

Day 43

Let's not forget what you read here several weeks ago—about God's plan for your life, His perfect timing, and the fact that one day with the Lord is like a thousand years.

I don't have the answer about why sometimes our prayers seem to go unanswered, but I do know this: My heavenly Father does listen to me, and He does know what's best for me today. Of course, He said it best in Matthew 6:34 (MSG).

> Give your entire attention to what God is doing right now, and don't get worked up about what may or may not happen tomorrow. God will help you deal with whatever hard things come up when the time comes.

Apparently God knows we are worrywarts! Here's another piece of His advice.

> Be careful for nothing; but in every thing by prayer and supplication with thanksgiving let your requests be made known unto God. And the peace of God, which passeth all understanding, shall keep your hearts and minds through Christ Jesus. (Philippians 4:6–7 KJV)

There's your answer to worry—it's prayer. In this instance, *careful* is *being full of care* or *anxious* or *worried*. Next we will look at some topics we should be praying about.

DAY 44

God desires that we spend time with Him every single day. Here are some specific items He has mentioned that we should be praying for in James 5:13–15 (MSG).

> Are you hurting? Pray. Do you feel great? Sing. Are you sick? Call the church leaders together to pray and anoint you with oil in the name of the Master. Believing-prayer will heal you, and Jesus will put you on your feet. And if you've sinned, you'll be forgiven—healed inside and out.

What if I'm sick and there are no church leaders I can call on? God made provision. Read the words of Jesus in Matthew 18:18–20 (KJV).

> Verily I say unto you, Whatsoever ye shall bind on earth shall be bound in heaven: and whatsoever ye shall loose on earth shall be loosed in heaven. Again I say until you, That if two of you shall agree on earth as touching any thing that they shall ask, it shall be done for them of my Father which is in heaven. For where two or three are gathered together in my name, there am I in the midst of them.

Ask a Christian friend to pray with you—it's okay to pray over the phone. That's still two gathered together in His name, and Jesus said He would be there. Aren't you glad that God thought of everything? Is there more? So glad you asked!

DAY 45

Have you ever thought, "What about when my friends want me to do something that I'm not sure about?" Prayer is the answer for that. Here's what Jesus had to say about it in Matthew 26:40–41 (MSG).

> When he came back to his disciples, he found them sound asleep. He said to Peter, "Can't you stick it out with me a single hour? Stay alert; be in prayer so you don't wander into temptation without even knowing you're in danger. There is a part of you that is eager, ready for anything in God. But there's another part that's as lazy as an old dog sleeping by the fire."

I'm broke and don't have the money to pay my bills. What now? Pray. Psalm 102:17 (NIRV) promises,

> He will answer the prayer of those who don't have anything. He won't say no to their cry for help.

Here's another prayer for your list from Matthew 5:44 (KJV):

> But I say unto you, Love your enemies, bless them that curse you, do good to them that hate you, and pray for them which despitefully use you, and persecute you.

Yuck! Did God really say to pray for those who hurt me? Yes, He did. How important is it for you to obey Him?

Day 46

And saving the best for last, here is the Lord's Prayer—the one that Jesus gave us to teach us how to pray—in Matthew 6:9–13 (TLB).

Pray along these lines:

"Our Father in heaven, we honor your holy name.

We ask that your kingdom will come now.

May your will be done here on earth, just as it is in heaven.

Give us our food again today, as usual, and

forgive us our sins, just as we have forgiven those who have sinned against us.

Don't bring us into temptation, but deliver us from the Evil One.

Amen."

DAY 47

Another way to help you build a relationship with our Lord is to read and study the Bible. After all, it is His book, and He gave it for a reason—and that's not to sit on a shelf.

There are many scriptures in this book, but they, alone, are not enough. You need the rest of the story.

A modern translation will help with your understanding and get beyond the *thee* and *thou* that can sometimes trip us up. But no matter which translation you can get your hands on, get one and use it. It's okay to write in the margins, underline verses, or highlight them when God reveals something to you.

Where do I start? For years all I read was the New Testament, thinking it was the only part of the Bible that was relevant to my life. Then I decided to accept a challenge to read through the Bible in one year. The schedule was to read from the Old Testament in the morning and from the New Testament in the evening. Wow! Was that an eye-opener? Suddenly all those passages I couldn't understand in the New Testament were clear.

Now I'll admit there were some parts of the Old Testament I had found boring—long lists of genealogies with names I couldn't pronounce, lists of the number of people in each tribe, and other details. Those are important to establish the order of our history, but I'll confess that I skimmed over them. So let's go back to the question, "Where do I start?"

Day 48

Where do I start? That's a tough question, and I'm not sure I have a correct answer. But let's read what God says.

> God means what he says. What he says goes. His powerful Word is sharp as a surgeon's scalpel, cutting through everything, whether doubt or defense, laying us open to listen and obey. Nothing and no one is impervious to God's Word. We can't get away from it—no matter what. (Hebrews 4:12 MSG)

So why did He write such a powerful book? Here's the answer in Psalm 33:11 (KJV):

> The counsel of the Lord standeth for ever, the thoughts of his heart to all generations.

Why do we need to know God's counsel (advice) and thoughts? That's how we learn His character—who He really is.

Is the Old Testament just that? Old and useless? Hardly. Read James 1:17 (KJV):

> Every good gift and every perfect gift is from above, and cometh down from the Father of lights, with whom is no variableness, neither shadow of turning.

If God never changes, then what He wrote in the Old Testament is for us! But what about Jesus and the New Testament? Read what He had to say.

DAY 49

Since Jesus is our example and the One we should follow, hear what He used when tempted by the devil in Matthew 4:4 (KJV):

> But he answered and said, It is written, Man shall not live by bread alone, but by every word that proceedeth out of the mouth of God.

He quoted Deuteronomy 8:3 from the Old Testament. Again, in Matthew 4:7 (KJV), still replying to the devil's temptations,

> Jesus said unto him, It is written again, Thou shalt not tempt the Lord thy God.

He was quoting Deuteronomy 6:16.

Then, a third time (the devil does not give up easily), Jesus rebuked him in Matthew 4:10 (KJV):

> Then saith Jesus unto him, Get thee hence, Satan: for it is written, Thou shalt worship the Lord thy God, and him only shalt thou serve.

Again he quoted from the Old Testament—Deuteronomy 6:13.

But look what happened in Matthew 4:11 (KJV):

> Then the devil leaveth him, and, behold, angels came and ministered unto him.

The devil gave up after hearing three verses from the Old Testament! This is Jesus; naturally He knew the Bible, but what about us? Does Jesus expect us to read the whole Bible?

Day 50

Some people called Jesus "Teacher." A teacher of what? The New Testament had not been written during the time while Jesus was on this earth. So when He spoke of scriptures, he was referring to the Old Testament.

When Jesus was challenged by the leaders in a town, he replied as it is written in Matthew 22:29 (KJV):

> Jesus answered and said unto them, Ye do err, not knowing the scriptures, nor the power of God.

So, yes, Jesus wants us to be knowledgeable about the entire book of God's Word—both Old and New Testaments. In fact, the Old Testament will open your eyes of understanding when reading the New Testament.

Back to that question—"Where do I start?"

.

Where you start depends on where you are—in your Christian walk, that is. If you've just accepted Jesus as your Lord and Savior, then start with the gospels, Matthew, Mark, Luke, and John. These books convey Jesus's words while here and his instructions.

Since Jesus is your teacher, it makes sense to know the instructions He left for you.

After you have read those four books, meditate. Meditate?

"What's this?" you may think. "I thought I was just reading."

Meditation is a great way to get God's Word stored up in your heart. Read a section and sit back and think about it. Ask God to give you a better understanding.

Then, after you have read and meditated on those four books, try other New Testament books like James or 1 John. Proverbs and Psalms from the Old Testament would come next. Then maybe you can return to the New Testament for some more instruction. Finally, tackle the Old Testament for a greater understanding of what you've been reading.

The entire Bible is a gift from God, and no matter how many times you've read a verse, it can reveal a new understanding. Reading, studying, and meditating on the Word of God are all adventures! You will begin to understand who He is and all He has done for you. Now get started!

Day 52

Are you alone? Need a friend? http://www.yourdictionary.com defines a friend as "someone who is on your side and with whom you talk or spend time." I feel that a friend is someone I can depend on, who isn't close one day and distant another.

I've found just such a friend and want to introduce you to Him—it's Jesus. Now before you say, "Get real!" and lay this book down, be patient with me.

Most of the people I consider friends were not true friends when I first met them—I had to get to know them before there was trust. The Bible gives us a look at friendship in Proverbs 18:24 (NIRV):

> A person with unfaithful friends soon comes to ruin. But
> there is a friend who sticks closer than a brother.

That makes it sound as if your choice of friends has a direct impact on your life. I've certainly found that to be true—have you? And since you can choose your friends, why not choose the friend "who sticks closer than a brother"? Let's get to know this Jesus.

Day 53

What's His background?

He is the only son of God. See John 3:16.

He was born in a stable with smelly sheep, donkeys, and cows—so He knows what being poor is all about. See Luke 2:6–7.

He and his parents had to flee their native land (because the ruler was killing all boy babies) and live in exile. He knows what it is to be afraid and alone in a new place. See Matthew 2:13.

His dad was a carpenter, and He worked in the shop with him. He knows what hard work is. See Mark 6:3.

He was a traveling preacher and knows what it means to be without a home. See Luke 9:58.

All His friends abandoned Him. He knows what rejection feels like. See Mark 14:50.

And He was mocked, spat on, beaten, and killed because people didn't like what He said. See Mark 15:16–20.

Hmm, sounds like He had a rough life, doesn't it? So how did He treat other people? Let's see.

Now that we know what we have—Jesus, this great High Priest with ready access to God—let's not let it slip through our fingers. We don't have a priest who is out of touch with our reality. He's been through weakness and testing, experienced it all—all but the sin. So let's walk right up to him and get what he is so ready to give. Take the mercy, accept the help.

Hebrews 4:14-16 (MSG)

Jesus was a teacher, but did He practice what He preached? Read one of the principles He taught in Matthew 7:1–2 (KJV):

> Judge not, that ye be not judged. For with what judgment ye judge, ye shall be judged: and with what measure ye mete, it shall be measured to you again.

He's telling us to quit being judge and jury when we see someone doing wrong. But Jesus was perfect—He never sinned, so how did He react to other people who did? We see one instance in John 8:3–11(KJV).

> And the scribes and Pharisees brought unto him a woman taken in adultery; and when they had set her in the midst, They say unto him, Master, this woman was taken in adultery, in the very act. Now Moses in the law commanded us, that such should be stoned: but what sayest thou? This they said, tempting him, that they might have to accuse him.

> But Jesus stooped down, and with his finger wrote on the ground, as though he heard them not. So when they continued asking him, he lifted up himself, and said unto them, He that is without sin among you, let him first cast a stone at her. And again he stooped down, and wrote on the ground.

> And they which heard it, being convicted by their own conscience, went out one by one, beginning at the eldest, even unto the last: and Jesus was left alone, and the woman standing in the midst. When Jesus had lifted up himself, and saw none but the woman, he said unto her. Woman, where are those thine accusers? Hath no man condemned thee? She said, No man, Lord.

> And Jesus said unto her, Neither do I condemn thee: go, and sin no more.

DAY 55

How about a friend who listens to you, even when busy, with lots of other people around?

Jesus did that in Mark 5:24b–34 (NIRV).

> A large group of people followed (Him). They crowded around him. A woman was there who had a sickness that made her bleed. It had lasted for 12 years. She had suffered a great deal, even though she had gone to many doctors. She had spent all the money she had. But she was getting worse, not better. Then she heard about Jesus. She came up behind him in the crowd and touched his clothes. She thought, "I just need to touch his clothes. Then I will be healed." Right away her bleeding stopped. She felt in her body that her suffering was over.
>
> At once Jesus knew that power had gone out from him. He turned around in the crowd. He asked, "Who touched my clothes?" "You see the people," his disciples answered, "They are crowding against you. And you still ask, 'Who touched me?'"
>
> But Jesus kept looking around. He wanted to see who had touched him. Then the woman came and fell at his feet. She knew what had happened to her. She was shaking with fear. But she told him the whole truth. He said to her, "Dear woman, your faith has healed you. Go in peace. You are free from your suffering."

He took the time to listen to her long story even though he was on his way somewhere else and surrounded by people.

Do you need a friend who will cry with you when you are sad or hurt? Jesus will do that.

He did it in the Bible when His friend Lazarus had died. But he wasn't crying because Lazarus died—Jesus was about to raise him from the dead! Why would He cry? No, He cried because He saw the pain that Martha and Mary, the dead man's sisters, were feeling.

Read John 11:32–36 (KJV).

> Then when Mary was come where Jesus was and saw him, she fell down at his feet, saying unto him, Lord, if thou hadst been here, my brother had not died. When Jesus therefore saw her weeping, and the Jews also weeping which came with her, he groaned in the spirit, and was troubled. And said, Where have ye laid him? They said unto him, Lord, come and see.
>
> Jesus wept.
>
> Then said the Jews, Behold how he loved him!

DAY 57

Do you know someone whom you consider your friend, but that person is always too busy for you? Not Jesus!

Read what He said in Matthew 28:20b (KJV):

> And, lo, I am with you always, even unto the end of the world. Amen."

Jesus said this only after telling those to whom He was speaking (true believers) to share the good news of who He was and instructing people how to live.

Another of His promises to be there always for you is found in John 14:18 (KJV):

> I will not leave you comfortless: I will come to you.

Now that's a loyal friend!

DAY 58

Some friends are just no fun—they must be serious all the time, but not Jesus! After He was crucified, His disciples were discouraged and returned to their former profession, fishing. They were sitting on the shore of Lake Galilee. The last thing they expected that day was a cookout on the beach! John 21:3–13 (KJV) tells this story.

> Simon Peter saith unto them, I go a fishing. They say unto him, We also go with thee. They went forth, and entered into a ship immediately: and that night they caught nothing.

> But when the morning was now come, Jesus stood on the shore: but the disciples knew not that it was Jesus. Then Jesus saith unto them, Children, have ye any meat? They answered him, No. And he said unto them, Cast the net on the right side of the ship, and ye shall find.

> They cast therefore, and now they were not able to draw it for the multitude of fishes. Therefore that disciple whom Jesus loved saith unto Peter, It is the Lord. Now when Simon Peter heard that it was the Lord, he girt his fisher's coat unto him, (for he was naked) and did cast himself into the sea.

> And the other disciples came in a little ship; (for they were not far from land, but as it were two hundred cubits,) dragging the net with fishes.

> As soon then as they were come to land, they saw a fire of coals there, and fish laid thereon, and bread.

> Jesus saith unto them, Bring of the fish which ye have now caught. Simon Peter went up, and drew the net to land full of great fishes, an hundred and fifty and three: and for all there were so many yet was not the net broken.

> Jesus saith unto them, Come and dine. And none of the disciples durst ask him, Who are thou? Knowing that it was the Lord. Jesus then cometh, and taketh bread, and giveth them, and fish likewise.

Do you ever feel down? Discouraged? Hopeless? A true friend is there to encourage you. That's what Jesus was doing when He was preparing His disciples for the time of His death. He offers the same encouragement for you. Read about it in John 16:33 (KJV):

> These things I have spoken unto you, that in me ye might have peace. In the world ye shall have tribulation: but be of good cheer; I have overcome the world.

Another time He encourages us in John 14:27 (TLB):

> I am leaving you with a gift—peace of mind and heart! And the peace I give isn't fragile like the peace the world gives. So don't be troubled or afraid.

It seems that Jesus wants His friends to have peace. Just this one characteristic makes me want to be friends with Him!

Day 60

Are you concerned about sharing your deepest thoughts with your friends because of what they might think of you? You can tell Jesus anything.

Read these verses.

> Don't fret or worry. Instead of worrying, pray. Let petitions and praises shape your worries into prayers, letting God know your concerns. Before you know it, a sense of God's wholeness, everything coming together for good, will come and settle you down. It's wonderful what happens when Christ displaces worry at the center of your life. (Philippians 4:6–7 MSG)

The same reassurance is in John 14:1 (KJV):

> Let not your heart be troubled: ye believe in God, believe also in me.

That reassurance is also in 1 Peter 5:7 (TLB):

> Let him have all your worries and cares, for he is always thinking about you and watching everything that concerns you.

Day 61

We all like friends who are there for us, don't judge us, and take the time to listen, but what about a friend who is totally honest with us? Sometimes we need a friend who will tell us when we are going down the wrong path. Trust Jesus for that!

Read John 15:11–15 (KJV).

> These things have I spoken unto you, that my joy might remain in you, and that your joy might be full.
>
> This is my commandment, That ye love one another, as I have loved you. Greater love hath no man than this, that a man lay down his life for his friends. Ye are my friends, if ye do whatsoever I command you. Henceforth I call you not servants: for the servant knoweth not what his lord doeth: but I have called you friends: for all things that I have heard of my Father I have made known unto you.

Now that's honest—maybe a bit more than we bargained for. So what has Jesus commanded you to do? It's all written in the Bible. Matthew, Mark, Luke, and John are all about Jesus and His commands but apparently not everything that He taught. Many of the books of the New Testament were written by those closest to Him while He was here; they were on the inside track and made sure those teachings were not lost. Jesus made certain you and I would have access to all He taught. It's there for the reading.

Day 62

But wait a minute. In that scripture yesterday, I read that I should put my life on the line for my friends. That's the kind of friend Jesus is? Yes, it is! Read about it in 1 Peter 1:18–21 (MSG).

> Your life is a journey you must travel with a deep consciousness of God. It cost God plenty to get you out of that dead-end, empty-headed life you grew up in. He paid with Christ's sacred blood, you know. He died like an unblemished, sacrificial lamb. And this was no afterthought. Even though it has only lately—at the end of the ages— become public knowledge, God always knew he was going to do this for you. It's because of this sacrificed Messiah, whom God then raised from the dead and glorified, that you trust God, that you know you have a future in God.

Hear more of the good news from your friend in Ephesians 1:7–10 (MSG).

> Because of the sacrifice of the Messiah, his blood poured out on the altar of the Cross, we're a free people—free of penalties and punishments chalked up by all our misdeeds. And not just barely free, either, Abundantly free! He thought of everything, provided for everything we could possibly need, letting us in on the plans he took such delight in making. He set it all out before us in Christ, a long-range plan in which everything would be brought together and summed up in him, everything in deepest heaven, everything on planet earth.

You have this kind of friend in Jesus!

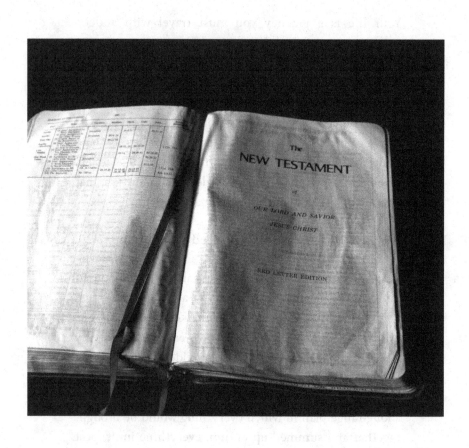

Day 63

Now we know what kind of friend Jesus is. What kind of friend are you? He gives us some answers on how to be the friends we should be in Matthew 11:28–30 (MSG).

> Are you tired? Worn out? Burned out on religion? Come to me. Get away with me and you'll recover your life. I'll show you how to take a real rest. Walk with me and work with me—watch how I do it. Learn the unforced rhythms of grace. I won't lay anything heavy or ill-fitting on you. Keep company with me and you'll learn to live freely and lightly.

Wow! Here is a friend who is willing to teach me how to be a friend. It's all there in the Bible. Here's a starter in 2 Corinthians 1:3–4 (KJV).

> Blessed be God, even the Father of our Lord Jesus Christ, the Father of mercies, and the God of all comfort; Who comforteth us in all our tribulations, that we may be able to comfort them which are in any trouble, by the comfort wherewith we ourselves are comforted of God.

There you have it. A friend for all the best reasons, who left a whole set of instructions for how to be His friend. Start with the gospels, Matthew, Mark, Luke, and John, to see how He lived on earth. Then do it—imitate Jesus!

Day 64

Okay, I'm learning about my new best friend, Jesus, but what do I do meanwhile? I'm finding it hard to do all this stuff. Here's some very good advice from Galatians 5:16–17 (TLB).

> I advise you to obey only the Holy Spirit's instructions. He will tell you where to go and what to do, and then you won't always be doing the wrong things your evil nature wants you to. For we naturally love to do evil things that are just the opposite from the things that the Holy Spirit tells us to do; and the good things we want to do when the Spirit has his way with us are just the opposite of our natural desires. These two forces within us are constantly fighting each other to win control over us, and our wishes are never free from their pressures.

Sometimes the wrong way and the right way are in that gray area, and it is so hard to tell the difference. God provided guidelines that give you a way to test your choices. The answer is found in Galatians 5:22–23 (NASB):

> But the fruit of the Spirit is love, joy, peace, patience, kindness, goodness, faithfulness, gentleness, self-control; against such things there is no law.

Will your choice give you any of these fruits?

Day 65

Let's look at each one of these fruits. We will start with serenity (peace).

The dictionary defines serenity as the state of being calm, peaceful, and untroubled. Oh, wow, that's the piece of fruit I want continually!

The first step is to have that peace in our relationship with Jesus, who sent us the Holy Spirit. Read Isaiah's prayer.

> Thou wilt keep him in perfect peace, whose mind is stayed
> on thee: because he trusteth in thee. Trust ye in the Lord
> for ever: for in the Lord Jehovah is everlasting strength.
> (Isaiah 26:3–4 KJV)

Notice that those verses instruct you to dedicate your heart and your mind to God. So the next time you are faced with a decision whose answers seem to be in the gray area, take a few minutes and dedicate your mind to God. Give Him time to guide you down the right path—you will know it's His guidance when you have that perfect peace.

What about those times when you try to dedicate your mind to God, but nothing happens? Take a look inside it to find the answer.

Day 66

What's inside your mind? It's full of whatever you have fed it, just as your body is full of the kinds of food you eat. The saying, "garbage in, garbage out" works with your mind as well. Our world is full of garbage, and it is very easy to fill our minds with it. What's the answer? Read Philippians 4:8 (KJV).

> Finally, brethren, whatsoever things are true, whatsoever things are honest, whatsoever things are just, whatsoever things are pure, whatsoever things are lovely, whatsoever things are of good report: if there be any virtue, and if there be any praise, think on these things.

Think about what TV shows you watch. Are they pure and wholesome? Or are they full of violence, sex, and bad language? Think about the books you read and ask yourself the same questions. I'm an avid reader and have several favorite authors. After practicing Philippians 4:8 for a while, one of those authors came out with a new book. I grabbed it and started reading. After the first few pages, I thought, "Has this author changed his whole style of writing?" No. I had changed my way of thinking. It was an eye-opener for me!

Day 67

Do your emotions run like a roller coaster? Roller coasters may be fun occasionally, but who wants to live on one? So how do we get those emotions back on an even track? Maybe a look at how we were created would be a good start. Read Psalm 139:13–14 (VOICE).

> For You shaped me, inside and out. You knitted me together
> in my mother's womb long before I took my first breath.
> I will offer You my grateful heart, for I am Your unique
> creation, filled with wonder and awe. You have approached
> even the smallest details with excellence; Your works are
> wonderful; I carry this knowledge deep within my soul.

That is wonderful news! I am a unique creation of God, filled with wonder and awe. Are you thinking, "I don't feel so wonderful right now because I've really messed up this unique creation of God"? There's more good news for you. Read Jude 1:24–25 (KJV).

> Now unto him that is able to keep you from falling, and
> to present you faultless before the presence of his glory
> with exceeding joy, To the only wise God our Saviour, be
> glory and majesty, dominion and power, both now and ever.
> Amen.

Yes, He made you a unique creation, and yes, He can keep you on your feet. That is the stuff emotional peace is made of!

Now I have peace—or rather I had peace until that certain someone walked by. That individual just knows how to push my buttons. I'm doing great in my Christian walk, and then something reminds me of that person, and peace goes right out the window. Surely I'm not the only one who has this problem. You're not alone! Since there are so many scriptures on enemies, God knew we would have these issues. Let's look at a few of those verses. See Romans 12:17–18 (MSG).

> Don't hit back; discover beauty in everyone. If you've got it in you, get along with everybody. Don't insist on getting even; that's not for you to do, "I'll do the judging," says God. "I'll take care of it."

It sounds like God knew it wouldn't be easy. Here's some more practical advice from Him in 1 Thessalonians 5:13–15 (MSG).

> Get along among yourselves, each of you doing your part. Our counsel is that you warn the freeloaders to get a move on. Gently encourage the stragglers, and reach out for the exhausted, pulling them to their feet. Be patient with each person, attentive to individual needs. And be careful that when you get on each other's nerves, you don't snap at each other. Look for the best in each other, and always do your best to bring it out.

I've done my part, but it just doesn't seem to work. My enemy is still my enemy and hurts me at every opportunity. Guess what? There's a verse for that. Read on.

Day 69

What's the answer for what I'm supposed to do, Lord, when people continue to hurt me? It's in Matthew 5:44 (KJV):

> But I say unto you, Love your enemies, bless them that curse you, do good to them that hate you, and pray for them which despitefully use you, and persecute you.

That's a big pill to swallow—love my enemies? How do I do that? Searching God's Word always gives me an answer. Here it is in Proverbs 25:21–22 (MSG).

> If you see your enemy hungry, go buy him lunch; if he's thirsty, bring him a drink. Your generosity will surprise him with goodness, and God will look after you.

There's the answer on love, but how about praying for those who hurt me? Just ask God to give you the words. It's hard at first, but as you continue to walk with Him, He will give you the path for prayer.

All this is to give me serenity? That sounds really good, but shouldn't there be more? Jesus answers that question in Matthew 5:9 (KJV):

> Blessed are the peacemakers: for they shall be called the children of God.

It's worth it all if I now have a place in God's family!

Day 70

It seems to me that all the fruits of the spirit are intertwined with each other. Just as a pot of soup isn't too tasty with just the broth, each time you add a vegetable, meat, or seasoning, it gets better until all the ingredients are added and it's complete. So it is with the Christian walk—every time we can add another fruit of the Spirit, we get better!

With that in mind, let's look at patience. Oh, brother, this is my challenge. When we look at the meaning of this word as used in the Bible, it is something like "enduring through difficult circumstances, or bearing up with courage."

Everyone's definition of *difficult* is different, but if it's difficult to you, then it's difficult.

We once waited on God's answer for ten years, but when it came, it was much more than we had ever thought or imagined! One verse we clung to during that wait was Psalm 40:1 (KJV):

> I waited patiently for the Lord: and he inclined unto me,
> and heard my cry.

We waited semipatiently! Did we give up and think we had missed God? Yes, for a bit. Did we try to make it happen? Yes, several times. Did that work? No, it failed miserably.

But our God is not semipatient—He is truly patient, and His timing is perfect. Now look at the rest of that passage.

What's the result of patience? Read it in Psalm 40:1–5a (KJV).

> I waited patiently for the Lord; and he inclined unto me, and heard my cry. He brought me up also out of an horrible pit, out of the miry clay, and set my feet upon a rock, and established my goings. And he hath put a new song in my mouth, even praise unto our God: many shall see it, and fear, and shall trust in the Lord. Blessed is that man that maketh the Lord his trust, and respecteth not the proud nor such as turn aside to lies. Many, O Lord my God, are thy wonderful works which thou hast done, and thy thoughts which are to us-ward.

Every word of that passage rings true to us—now. But during the wait? We heard all the negative comments—like "You've lost your mind." My own mother said, "I didn't know you were that smart," after she saw what God had done.

Do we have this issue of patience down? Apparently we do not because we are in the middle of another wait!

Day 72

What else is this ability to wait good for? We found out in Isaiah 40:31 (KJV).

> But they that wait upon the Lord shall renew their strength;
> they shall mount up with wings as eagles; they shall run,
> and not be weary; and they shall walk, and not faint.

Patience is not only waiting for an answer from God. Patience is "enduring through difficult circumstances." Now that's tough patience.

The first step of enduring is to give the situation over to God and then do it over again tomorrow, the following day, and the day after that.

The verse above tells us we will gain new strength. What? It's all I can do to endure each day. That strength comes when we begin seeking God and His strength through prayer and searching His Word for answers.

Pray for God to give you strength. It's okay to tell Him if you feel weak and unable to go on. Remember that He hears your prayers. Then begin searching His Word.

Read on for some help.

Day 73

Reading Christian books may help your understanding of some issues, but the true source of God's wisdom is in His Word. Here's a verse to help when you are enduring a difficult time.

> So, brothers and sisters, all you need to do now is stand firm and hold tight to the line of teachings we have passed on to you . . . Now may our Lord Jesus (the Anointed One Himself) and God our Father (who has loved us, comforted us eternally, and given us a good hope by His grace) bring comfort to your hearts and strengthen your wills to accomplish every good work and word. (2 Thessalonians 2:15–17 VOICE)

Hold tight? Does that mean you have to carry your Bible in your hand wherever you go? Not quite. Hold God's Word tightly in your heart and mind. To do that, whenever you find a verse that really jumps out at you— that gives you hope—read it repeatedly until you have it memorized.

When you have some verses of God's Word memorized, then no matter where you are or how far away your Bible is, you can stand firmly and know that He is right there with you. He is giving you strength for that moment when you need it the most.

The other half of patience is long-suffering. Sometimes I want to erase that word. *Long* and *suffering*? Put those together in one word, and it sounds like a huge pothole in the path of the Christian life.

When I dug a little deeper into the original meaning of the word, it surprised me. It really refers to your frame of mind during difficult times. When you put together patience, which means endurance, and long-suffering, which refers to your frame of mind while enduring, it sounds as if God knew we would have difficult times and is giving us some help.

But first a caution: Don't we all like to share our troubles with others, hoping they will empathize with us? Have you ever found that, while sharing with a friend, the more you tell, the more angry you become? Read James 3:5–6 (MSG).

> It only takes a spark, remember, to set off a forest fire. A careless or wrongly placed word out of your mouth can do that. By our speech we can ruin the world, turn harmony to chaos, throw mud on a reputation, send the whole world up in smoke and go up in smoke with it, smoke right from the pit of hell.

Long-suffering also includes keeping our emotions quiet, and that comes much more easily when we don't gossip about those who hurt us.

Day 75

Ouch! *Long-suffering* sounds as if God is asking you to do something really difficult while you are going through difficult times. Double difficulty? No.

Entering that frame of mind for endurance requires you to keep God close by. How better to do that than stay in His Word? Reading puts the words in your mind, but meditating (reading over again and thinking about it for a while) puts it into your heart. So work on it from the top down—from your head to your heart.

As I was searching the Bible for words of encouragement, there were so many that I think it's worth spending time just meditating on them. Here are a couple to get you started. I encourage you to keep digging!

Philippians 4:13 (KJV):

> I can do all things through Christ which strengtheneth me.

1 John 4:4 (KJV):

> Ye are of God, little children, and have overcome them: because greater is he that is in you, than he that is in the world.

Day 76

Among the fruits of the Spirit are kindness and goodness. Are these automatic when we receive Jesus and the Holy Spirit? Yes, but let me explain.

The attributes of the Holy Spirit living within you are referred to as fruits for a reason.

You don't go out one day and see a ripe peach on a tree that wasn't there the day before, do you? First a seed had to be planted, and that seed grew into a little sapling. Then the tree grew, and when it became mature enough, it began to blossom. Those blossoms turned into tiny fruits that were not yet edible. Finally, after a while, the fruit grew ripe, ready to be eaten and nourish someone.

Along the way, someone had to care for the tree. It needed water, food, sunlight, and maybe even a rod to be sure it grew straight.

It takes work to produce fruit on a tree, just as it does to produce the fruits of the Spirit. To clear room for all that fruit, we sometimes need to clean house, and some of the former things in our lives have to go. Read 2 Corinthians 5:17 (KJV):

> Therefore if any man be in Christ, he is a new creation: old things are passed away; behold all things are become new.

Let's look at what a little sapling needs to grow into maturity.

Day 77

The Holy Spirit planted seeds within you when you accepted Jesus as Savior and received the Holy Spirit. All of us have been saplings at some time. We needed food to grow, so we fed on the Word of God. Reading and meditating on the Bible will feed your spirit.

All plants need water and where do we get that? Find out in John 4:13–14 (KJV).

> Jesus answered and said unto her, Whosoever drinketh of this water shall thirst again: But whosoever drinketh of the water that I shall give him shall never thirst; but the water that I shall give him shall be in him a well of water springing up into everlasting life.

Spending time with Jesus in prayer will water your growing tree with the purest, most wonderful water anywhere. I don't know about you, but I leak—so I keep going back for more!

That rod to keep a tree straight doesn't sound like fun, but it will make you into a straight, strong tree, able to stand up to frequent storms. Read Proverbs 19:20 (KJV):

> Hear counsel, and receive instruction, that thou mayest be wise in thy latter end."

Now that we are on the way to a beautiful, strong tree that's ready to bear fruit, let's get back to kindness and goodness. What's the difference? One is what you do, and the other is what you are.

The Bible always uses the phrase "show kindness," meaning people did something. Here are three examples.

> Then said David, I will shew kindness unto Hanun the son of Nahash, as his father shewed kindness unto me. And David sent to comfort him by the hand of his servants for his father. And David's servants came into the land of the children of Ammon. (2 Samuel 10:2 KJV)

> But shew kindness unto the sons of Barzillai the Gileadite, and let them be of those that eat at thy table: for so they came to me when I fled because of Absalom thy brother. (1 Kings 2:7 KJV)

> And the barbarous people shewed us no little kindness: for they kindled a fire, and received us every one, because of the present rain, and because of the cold. (Acts 28:2 KJV)

In the first two instances of "showing kindness," the people were repaying a kindness done to them with a kindness to someone else. One comforted a man who had lost his father. The other's kindness was in asking for protection and food. The third verse showed kindness to strangers who had been shipwrecked. They built a fire to keep them warm. Kindness can be a wide range of actions—feeding people, offering sympathy, helping strangers feel welcome. All were actions. To show kindness, you must do something.

If kindness is what you do, then goodness is what you are. A person of goodness stands up for what is right. Because good people believe in what is right, their lives reflect right living.

Of course, our best example of a good person is Jesus. He showed thousands of acts of kindness, but He was also filled with goodness. He had a clear handle on what was right, and He meant it. A good example of standing up for what is right can be found in John 2:13–17 (VOICE).

> The time was near to celebrate the Passover, the festival commemorating when God rescued His children from slavery in Egypt, so Jesus went to Jerusalem for the celebration. Upon arriving, He entered the temple to worship. But the porches and colonnades were filled with merchants selling sacrificial animals (such as doves, oxen, and sheep) and exchanging money. Jesus fashioned a whip of cords and used it with skill driving out animals; He scattered the money and overturned the tables, emptying profiteers from the house of God. There were dove merchants still standing around, and Jesus reprimanded them.
>
> Jesus: What are you still doing here? Get all your stuff and haul it out of here! Stop making My Father's house a place for your own profit! The disciples were astounded but they remembered that the Hebrew Scriptures said, "Jealous devotion for God's house consumes me."

God's house was to be honored and filled with awe for Him—it was not for making profit by cheating people. Jesus's zeal for what was right couldn't be contained.

Day 80

Another fruit of the Spirit is faithfulness. One of the definitions of being faithful or having faithfulness is, "steady in allegiance or affection, loyal, constant." I don't think this fruit is our allegiance to our favorite pro team but our faithfulness to God.

All the fruits reflect that God's character and faithfulness are no exceptions. As it is written in 1 John 1:9 (KJV):

> If we confess our sins, he is faithful and just to forgive us our sins, and to cleanse us from all unrighteousness.

This principle is also revealed in 1 Corinthians 1:9 (VOICE):

> God is faithful and in His faithfulness called you out into an intimate relationship with His Son, our Lord Jesus the Anointed.

You've taken the first step in believing. Will you take the next step toward faithfulness to God? Faithfulness to Him is staying loyal to His Word and praying for His direction. That will change your life. It's your choice.

Day 81

I think two other fruits are ones that must go together. They are gentleness and self-control.

Read Philippians 4:5 (VOICE):

> Keep your gentle nature so that all people will know what it looks like to walk in His footsteps. The Lord is ever present with us.

What is *gentle*? The dictionary defines it as "free from harshness, sternness, or violence" or not needing to force our way.

That definition indicates that we need a little self-control, doesn't it? Perhaps that's why these two fruits are listed together.

I love this definition of self-control as our ability to direct our energies wisely. Easier said than done, right? How do we learn this kind of self-control? Read James 1:19–21 (VOICE).

> Listen, open your ears, harness your desire to speak, and don't get worked up into a rage so easily, my brothers and sisters. Human anger is a futile exercise that will never produce God's kind of justice in this world. So walk out on your corrupt liaison with smut and depraved living, and humbly welcome the word of truth that will blossom like the seed of salvation planted in your souls.

Wow! It's not a matter of teaching yourself how *not* to get angry—it's the fact that staying in the Word of God changes you so that irritating events don't make you so angry any more.

Now we come to joy. The Message version of the Bible calls it "exuberance about life." Do you feel great enthusiasm and excitement about your life? If not, read what the Bible offers. I had a hard time trying to decide which verses on joy to share because there are so many. This is just a sample. The first is in Proverbs 10:28 (VOICE):

> The hope of those who do right is joy and celebration, but the only prospect for those who do wrong is futility.

Now we go to Romans 15:13 (KJV):

> May the God of hope fill you with all joy and peace in believing, that ye may abound in hope, through the power of the Holy Ghost.

The benefits of joy? One is found in Proverbs 17:22 (AMP):

> A happy heart is a good medicine and a joyful mind causes healing, but a broken spirit dries up the bones.

One more in Nehemiah 8:10b (KJV):

> Neither be ye sorry; for the joy of the Lord is your strength.

This scripture brings us to the first fruit on the list and the greatest—that is love.

Day 83

"Love never fails." What? You haven't met my boss, or my ex, or that guy who lives next door. But those three words come straight out of 1 Corinthians 13:8 (NIV), so they must be the truth, right? Let's look at the verses just before that as they describe what this kind of love is.

> Love is patient and kind. Love is not jealous or boastful or proud or rude. It does not demand its own way. It is not irritable, and it keeps no record of being wronged. It does not rejoice about injustice but rejoices whenever the truth wins out. Love never gives up, never loses faith, is always hopeful and endures through every circumstance. (1 Corinthians 13:4–7 NLT)

Did you see anything about liking someone? No, because this kind of love is a choice—not a feeling. You choose to show all those attitudes toward everyone. Easy? No. Worth it? Yes, because it never fails.

Now go back and reread the verses as if you are the recipient of that kind of love. You are, you know. God made a choice to love you. Shouldn't you make that same one?

Day 84

Where do we get the idea that God actually chose us to love? He told us so—in His Word. Read Ephesians 1:4–5 (TLB).

> Long ago, even before he made the world, God chose us to be his very own through what Christ would do for us; he decided then to make us holy in his eyes, without a single fault—we who stand before him covered with his love. His unchanging plan has always been to adopt us into his own family by sending Jesus Christ to die for us. And he did this because he wanted to!

Well, that was a long time ago. Does He still love us after we've made such a mess of His world? You've heard this before, but hear it again and again until it's buried deep in your heart.

> For I am persuaded, that neither death, nor life, nor angels, nor principalities, nor powers, nor things present, nor things to come, Nor height, nor depth, nor any other creature, shall be able to separate us from the love of God, which is in Christ Jesus our Lord. (Romans 8:38–39 KJV)

Maybe we should look more closely into a God who loves us that much!

We serve a powerful God. Just look around you at the creations not made by humans. He created them all!

Let's look at some of the verses about His power, first in Isaiah 40:26 (VOICE).

> Look at the myriad of stars and constellations above you. Who set them to burning, each in its place? Who knows those countless lights each by name? They obediently shine each in its place, because God has the great strength and strong power to make it so.

Read Jeremiah 32:17 (KJV):

> Ah Lord God! behold, thou hast made the heaven and the earth by thy great power and stretched out arm, and there is nothing too hard for thee."

Nothing is too hard for God? No, not even your hardest problem.

> God's Son shines out with God's glory, and all that God's Son is and does marks him as God. He regulates the universe by the mighty power of his command. He is the one who died to cleanse us and clear our record of all sin, and then sat down in highest honor beside the great God of heaven. (Hebrews 1:3 TLB)

There's proof of His great love for you.

God is also a holy God. He can do no wrong. We can worship Him freely because we know He isn't going to make a mistake somewhere down the road. Consider 1 Samuel 2:2 (KJV).

> There is none holy as the Lord: for there is none besides thee: neither is there any rock like our God.

Then read Isaiah 6:3b (KJV).

> Holy, holy, holy is the Lord of hosts: the whole earth is full of his glory.

But if we serve such a holy God, what does that require of us? It's in 1 Peter 1:13–16 (KJV).

> Wherefore gird up the loins of your mind, be sober, and hope to the end for the grace that is to be brought unto you at the revelation of Jesus Christ; As obedient children, not fashioning yourselves according to the former lusts in your ignorance: But as he which hath called you is holy, so be ye holy in all manner of conversation; Because it is written, Be ye holy; for I am holy.

This scripture shows that being holy doesn't happen instantly. The verse says to let ourselves be pulled into a way of life shaped by God's life. It's like pulling out a car stuck in mud to dry ground—it takes time and effort! That's why we need a God who is always there to help.

Day 87

God doesn't just sit on a throne in heaven and never look down at us. He's always at your side. Study the scriptures that tell us this.

> Am I a God at hand, saith the Lord, and not a God afar off? Can any hide himself in secret places that I shall not see him? Saith the Lord. Do not I fill heaven and earth? Saith the Lord. (Jeremiah 23:23–24 KJV)

Read Psalm 46:1 (KJV):

> God is our refuge and strength, a very present help in trouble.

Here's instruction with a promise.

> Let your conversation be without covetousness; and be content with such things as ye have for he hath said, I will never leave thee, nor forsake thee. So that we may boldly say, The Lord is my helper, and I will not fear what man shall do unto me? (Hebrews 13:5–6 KJV)

And then this promise from Psalm 136:1–3 (KJV):

> O give thanks unto the Lord; for he is good: for his mercy endureth for ever, O give thanks unto the God of gods: for his mercy endureth for ever, O give thanks to the Lord of lords: for his mercy endureth for ever.

His mercy? His loving kindness—the kind of love we don't deserve—goes on forever.

You can depend on Him because He is faithful and full of mercy, as it is written in 1 John 1:9 (KJV):

> If we confess our sins, he is faithful and just to forgive us our sins, and to cleanse us from all unrighteousness.

Psalm 119:90 (KJV) assures us of His commitment:

> Thy faithfulness is unto all generations: thou hast established the earth, and it abideth."

For those times when everything seems hopeless, read Lamentations 3:21–24 (KJV).

> This I recall to my mind, therefore have I hope. It is of the Lord's mercies that we are not consumed, because his compassions fail not, They are new every morning: great is thy faithfulness. The Lord is my portion, saith my soul; therefore will I hope in him.

When you feel this way, it's time to have a good talk with Him. What can be done with your life? Don't give up on it—God hasn't! Go to the next page.

Day 89

When you feel alone, try this exercise. Read about it in Romans 12:12 (MSG).

> So here's what I want you to do, God helping you. Take your everyday ordinary life—your sleeping, eating, going-to-work, and walking-around life—and place it before God as an offering. Embracing what God does for you is the best thing you can do for him without even thinking. Instead, fix your attention on God. You'll be changed from the inside out. Readily recognize what he wants from you, and quickly respond to it. Unlike the culture around you, always dragging you down to its level of immaturity, God brings the best out of you, develops well-formed maturity in you.

This exercise works! But it takes action—give your life to Him, accept what God does for you, and fix your attention on Him. Give it a try.

Moses asked God a question about what to say if someone asked what God's name was. God answered in Exodus 3:14 (KJV):

> And God said unto Moses, I Am That I Am: and he said, Thus shalt thou say unto the children of Israel, I Am hath sent me unto you.

Notice God didn't say, "I was" or "I will be." He said "I AM." He is the God of today—there for you every minute of every day.

DAY 90

David was a man after God's heart. As a boy, he was the family's shepherd of their flock of sheep. He spent hours and hours with those sheep and knew them well. Have you ever wondered why he used a shepherd as the metaphor for God and sheep as the metaphor for us when he wrote Psalm 23?

I did some research on sheep, and while I am certainly no expert, I did find some interesting points about them. They are social animals—they like to be with other sheep. They can recognize faces and remember them. They can learn the sound of a person's voice. As we can read in John 10:14–15 (KJV), Jesus also used sheep as examples when He taught.

> I am the good shepherd, and know my sheep, and am
> known of mine. As the Father knoweth me, even so know I
> the Father: and I lay down my life for the sheep.

On the other hand, sheep are not the brightest animals in the barnyard. They need a shepherd. So let's take a look at Psalm 23, verse by verse. Psalm 23:1 (NIV):

> The Lord is my shepherd. I lack nothing.

I lack nothing? Yes, you only need one shepherd—Jesus—to care for you, love you, and forgive you when you go the wrong way. He's always there—just a whisper away.

DAY 91

Continuing with Psalm 23:2 (NIV):

> He makes me lie down in green pastures, he leads me beside
> quiet waters.

Notice the pastures are green—not rocky and rough, not dried up and full of dead grass. That takes work on the shepherd's part. For lambs to gain weight and grow, they need lush pastures where they can munch for a few hours and then lie down and rest. They can't be constantly wandering around, hunting for a few blades of grass here and there.

The shepherd must provide a fertile field for his sheep. Then he can sit back and watch his sheep as they rest in that lush grass, contented with their master's food.

We can munch on the Word of God, which will cause us to gain spiritual weight, grow to maturity, and be content when we lie down at night—no matter where that is.

Why quiet waters? Why lead instead of just letting the sheep find it? That's for tomorrow—and the next day!

In peace I will lie down and sleep, for you alone,
Lord, make me dwell in safety.
Psalm 4:8 (NIV)

Sheep are good followers. They know their shepherd's voice and will gladly follow him wherever he leads them. What? I don't think so! Let's see—what about Isaiah 53:6 (TLB)?

> We—every one of us—have strayed away like sheep! We, who left God's paths to follow our own. Yet God laid on him the guilt and sins of every one of us!

Ouch! That stung a bit—but sometimes we need to hear the truth. Yup—we are like sheep.

Sheep can learn to recognize their shepherd's voice, and they remember it, but sometimes the grass looks a little greener in the other direction. Have you ever heard the voice of Jesus calling you to follow Him and strayed anyway? You're not alone. That's why Jesus said, "I am the good Shepherd; I know my sheep."

Read what else Jesus said in Luke 15:3–7 (KJV).

> And he spake this parable unto them, saying, What man of you, having an hundred sheep, if he lose one of them, doth not leave the ninety and nine in the wilderness and go after that which is lost, until he find it? And when he hath found it, he layeth it on his shoulders, rejoicing. And when he cometh home, he calleth together his friends and neighbours, saying unto them, Rejoice with me; for I have found my sheep which was lost. I say unto you, that likewise joy shall be in heaven over one sinner that repenteth, more than over ninety and nine just persons, which need no repentance.

DAY 93

Psalm 23:2 (NIV):

> He makes me lie down in green pastures, he leads me beside
> quiet waters.

Why quiet waters? Sheep are afraid of loud, rushing, water. They prefer the calm of a quiet stream. Do you see the similarities? There are times when the chaos of everyday living makes me want to retreat to a quiet place and just enjoy the peace.

But can I find the quiet waters—peace—on my own? No—I must choose to follow Him.

In New Zealand we had the privilege of watching a few shepherds leading over a thousand sheep down the highway to greener pastures. They had to cross a bridge to get there. Most of the sheep had crossed the bridge when a car came along behind them, scaring a few stragglers. Instead of following the shepherd when they were frightened, they all turned and ran away from their leader and back across the bridge. The shepherds had to go back to them, calm them down, and then lead them back across the bridge once again.

Sound familiar? Have you been following Jesus, getting along well, and then something happens that scares you, and you turn and run? Go back to yesterday and read Luke 15:3–7.

Did those New Zealand shepherds give up on their sheep? No, they went after them, just as Jesus does—always there to comfort and carry you back to safety.

Psalm 23:3 (NIV):

> He refreshes my soul. He guides me along the right paths
> for his name's sake.

Notice that the verb is *refreshes*, not *refreshed*. He gives our souls continuous refreshment, over and over again. That *aah* of amazement, joy, or surprise is refreshing.

If I follow Him, He guides me along the right paths. The original Hebrew word for *path* referred to something like a rut. A rut doesn't usually form the first time a wagon rolls over the ground. It takes time, work, and rolling over the same spot several times. In this case, it's okay for you to be in a rut!

"For His name's sake," the psalmist specifies. Do you think a shepherd spends all that time each day taking care of sheep for their sake? No—they are there for the shepherd's benefit. Likewise, God has created us for His name's sake—His benefit. We bring glory to His name—but only when we stay in that rut. What does staying in that rut mean for you? We've already found several benefits—now let's look at more.

DAY 95

P salm 23:4a (NIV):

> Even though I walk through the darkest valley, I will fear
> no evil, for you are with me.

Have you ever had to walk through a dark valley? Someone walks out on you, your world falls apart, the judge bangs his gavel, or your kids are on drugs—or maybe you are. We each have our own valleys. Valleys are always surrounded by high mountains that look impossible to climb.

So how can you get to this point of "I will fear no evil"?

Focus on Jesus's words in John 16:33 (KJV):

> These things I have spoken unto you, that in me ye might
> have peace. In the world ye shall have tribulation: but be of
> good cheer; I have overcome the world.

Jesus has already won the battle! And that same Jesus lives within anyone who invites Him in. He knows when you have trouble—He told us a long time ago that we would have it—but He also gives us peace while going through that trouble. Stay in your rut!

Psalm 23:4b (NIV) informs us,

> Your rod and your staff, they comfort me.

A shepherd always carried both a rod and a staff. The rod wasn't metal like many rods today. It was a wooden stick. This rod could be used both for defense and offense.

Obviously, the defensive role of the rod was to keep predators away from the herd. That's comforting in itself. Knowing you are being protected from potential harm gives you peace.

Offensively? A wandering sheep could be struck—not beaten—with the tip of the rod when it decided to take off on its own. Thank God that we have a Savior who will lead us back when we wander off!

The staff was a long wooden pole with a crook at the end. Once again, when a sheep got into trouble, perhaps by falling off a ledge or getting caught in brambles, the shepherd could put the crook part of the staff gently around the sheep's neck and pull it back to safety.

Do you notice the similarity between a rod and a staff? They protect us when we are in danger—but also when we start off on the wrong path. You can never wander so far from Jesus that you can't repent and return.

DAY 97

As if the first four verses weren't enough, there's still more! Continue with Psalm 23:5 (NIV):

> You prepare a table before me in the presence of my enemies.
> You anoint my head with oil; my cup overflows.

In this verse, *table* refers to a spread or feast. And look who is preparing it—the God of the universe! He lays out before you food, water, protection, loving kindness even when you stray, peace and comfort in times of trouble—and the list goes on. He does this in front of your enemies, and they can't do anything about it. Then that anointing? Read about it in Psalm 45:7 (NIV):

> You love righteousness and hate wickedness; therefore
> God, your God, has set you above your companions by
> anointing you with the oil of joy.

All this and joy also? How can your cup not overflow? Will you ever feel the same again about being compared to a sheep? But there's one more verse.

DAY 98

The last verse is Psalm 23:6 (NIV):

> Surely your goodness and love will follow me all the days
> of my life, and I will dwell in the house of the Lord forever.

This is the result of following the lead of the great shepherd, Jesus. Have you ever looked behind you at your past and seen only regret and sorrow?

Now you have something new following you. It's the goodness and love of God. It's so pure and holy that, when you look back, you can't even see all that garbage, which is now behind the goodness and love of God.

Lean back into that goodness of God. He will give you the strength to follow. Feel the warmth of His love and then look at the last phrase for the best of all promises, "I will dwell in the house of the Lord forever."

You—yes, you—will dwell in the house of the Lord forever. What's that house going to be like? A glimpse is in Revelation 21:4 (KJV):

> And God shall wipe away all tears from their eyes; and
> there shall be no more death, neither sorrow, nor crying,
> neither shall there be any more pain: for the former things
> are passed away.

That sounds like heaven to me.

DAY 99

For the past nine days, we have been looking at Psalm 23. It has six verses. This is a good example of how to meditate on God's Word. We could have read those six verses in a few minutes. However, when we delved into the meaning and let God show us what He meant when He instructed David to write it, we found so much more.

When you find yourself in a seemingly impossible situation, ask Jesus to help you see a way out—and He will. Will you now remember that shepherd's staff with the crook on the end? Can you see Him gently tugging you out of the briars?

Read Psalm 40:1–2 (KJV).

> I waited patiently for the Lord; and he inclined unto me,
> and heard my cry. He brought me up also out of an horrible
> pit, out of the miry clay, and set my feet upon a rock, and
> established my goings.

How does He steady you? Through His Word and through prayer time spent alone with Him. As you spend more time in His Word, you will be steadied and make right choices. Are you ready for that?

Let's start with right choices. I've made plenty of wrong choices and have always regretted them. We have a God who made the choice to love you and me no matter what we do. But then he gave us a life of free choices. From the good choices come blessings, and from the bad choices come regret. I'll take blessings over regret any day!

Joshua made this division very clear to his people.

> And if it seem evil unto you to serve the Lord, choose you this day whom ye will serve; whether the gods which your fathers served that were on the other side of the flood, or the gods of the Amorites, in whose land ye dwell: but as for me and my house, we will serve the Lord. (Joshua 24:15 KJV)

It's your choice. When we accept Jesus as our Lord and Savior and his promise of eternal life, it's not enough to view Him as a fire escape from hell. Your choices took on a new light from the time you accepted Him into your heart. How do we serve the Lord? By making the right choices. To learn how to do that, the direction is in Psalm 25:12 (AMP).

> Who is the man who fears the Lord (with awe-inspired reverence and worships Him with submissive wonder)? He will teach him (through His word) in the way he should choose.

Let's look at some of those choices.

Day 101

Which choice shall we examine first? Choices begin in the mind, so let's start with our thought life. Read Proverbs 23:7a (KJV):

> For as he thinketh in his heart, so is he.

Since we are considering thoughts, what are you thinking right now? What thoughts dominate most of your waking time? Do you think of how someone has hurt you? Or are you thinking of how you can get even with someone? How about trying to come up with a way to make that person know how evil he or she really is—what clever thing you can say the next time you meet up with that person? That's not God's way. Here's what He says in Philippians 4:8 (TLB).

> Let me say this one more thing: Fix your thoughts on what
> is true and good and right. Think about things that are pure
> and lovely, and dwell on the fine, good things in others.
> Think about all you can praise God for and be glad about.

Whoa! That's a boatload of thoughts to take in. How am I supposed to switch off these bad thoughts and turn on the good thoughts? You already have the answer in that switch! Read on.

Choices are there not only for thoughts but for switches—like the one on your TV. What do you watch? Violence? Sex? Filthy language? Yes, I know it's on every channel. It's the way of the world, but you are not of this world any longer.

There are channels that offer old TV series, game shows, travel shows, educational shows, and informative programs. Do these sound boring? I thought so too—until I made myself watch a few. The result? One evening I went back to the shows I had watched in the past and suddenly found them so violent and full of bad language that I turned the television off. They hadn't changed—I had!

It's your choice—use that switch on your TV and keep remembering Philippians 4:8 (TLB):

> Fix your thoughts on what is true and good and right.
> Think about things that are pure and lovely.

The definition of *fix* is to direct one's eyes, mind, or attention steadily or unwaveringly toward a target or objective.

Keep thinking of what is true and good and right and pure and lovely over and over. Okay, we have that TV switched to a different mode. Now let's look at other thoughts.

Your choice switch works the same with what you read and the music you hear. Remember that you are in control of the switch. It's your choice. Pay attention to what Jesus said in Matthew 6:22-23 (TLB).

> If your eye is pure, there will be sunshine in your soul. But if your eye is clouded with evil thoughts and desires, you are in deep spiritual darkness. And oh, how deep that darkness can be!

Let's move on to what those thoughts about people are like. This is my most difficult task. I pass someone who has caused me hurt, and I think, "What a tacky outfit. She has no taste in fashion at all." Or I see a group laughing and wonder if it's about me.

Then I learned to use the five-second rule. Remember, if a piece of food hits the floor and you pick it up in five seconds, it's okay to eat? Try the five-second rule on your thought life. When one of those unkind thoughts comes in, get rid of it within five seconds, and your mind stays cleaner! It's a habit worth keeping.

I want to stay in the sunshine Jesus talked about in Matthew. So we are cleaning up the thoughts; what's next? That's for tomorrow.

Do your mouth and what comes out of it ever get you into trouble? Apparently you are not alone! Read James 3:8–14 (VOICE).

> But no man has ever demonstrated the ability to tame his own tongue! It is a spring of restless evil, brimming with toxic poisons. Ironically this same tongue can be both an instrument of blessing to our Lord and Father and a weapon that hurls curses upon others who are created in God's own image. One mouth streams forth both blessings and curses. My brothers and sisters, this is not how it should be. Does a spring gush crystal clear freshwater and moments later spurt out bitter salt water? My brothers and sisters, does a fig tree produce olives? Is there a grapevine capable of growing figs? Can salt water give way to freshwater?
>
> Who in your community is understanding and wise? Let his example, which is marked by wisdom and gentleness, blaze a trail for others. If your heart is one that bleeds dark streams of jealousy and selfishness, do not be so proud that you ignore your depraved state.

I guess our words have gotten us in trouble for thousands of years, but don't words come from our thoughts? If so, it's another reason to get thoughts under control.

Day 105

I think the choices most visible to others are our possessions. Those choices are hard to hide! What do they say about you? Focus on what Jesus had to say about possessions in Luke 12:15 (NIV):

> Then he said to them, Watch out! Be on your guard against all kinds of greed; life does not consist in an abundance of possessions.

It seems that Jesus meant for our focus to be on something more permanent, doesn't it? Hear Him again in Matthew 6:19–21 (KJV).

> Lay not up for yourselves treasures upon earth, where moth and rust doth corrupt, and where thieves break through and steal: But lay up for yourselves treasures in heaven, where neither moth nor rust doth corrupt, and where thieves do not break through and steal: For where your treasure is, there will your heart be also.

Think about this: Do your possessions own you and dictate your time, or do you own your possessions and use them wisely?

Even though the choice of our possessions is important, what we desire could be an even greater choice. Have you ever seen an ad on TV for new cars that said, "When your present car wears out and won't run anymore, come see us"? No way! They always show a car that's a bit better than the one you have or does more—or has more cup holders. They mean to give you a desire for their product. Read 1 John 2:15–17 (KJV) on possessions.

> Love not the world, neither the things that are in the world.
> If any man love the world, the love of the Father is not in
> him. For all that is in the world, the lust of the flesh, and
> the lust of the eyes, and the pride of life, is not of the Father,
> but is of the world. And the world passeth away, and the lust
> thereof: but he that doeth the will of God abideth for ever.

Those desires can also be totally destructive. Focus on the wisdom in 1 Timothy 6:9 (TLB).

> But people who long to be rich soon begin to do all kinds
> of wrong things to get money, things that hurt them and
> make them evil-minded and finally send them to hell itself.

Our desires can lead us to make the wrong choice of action. But there's more. That's for tomorrow.

Day 107

We've talked about doing good earlier, but just doing good deeds may not be enough. How are you at work? We know that God is ever present—and that means on the job. He gave instructions for that also. Read them in Colossians 3:22–25 (MSG).

> Servants, do what you're told by your earthly masters. And don't just do the minimum that will get you by. Do your best. Work from the heart for your real Master, for God, confident that you'll get paid in full when you come into your inheritance. Keep in mind always that the ultimate Master you're serving is Christ. The sullen servant who does shoddy work will be held responsible. Being a follower of Jesus doesn't cover up bad work.

Okay, so I'll do what the boss says—grumble, grumble, grumble. Hold on a minute—where did that attitude come from? Need an attitude check? Meditate on Ephesians 4:21–23 (VOICE).

> If you have heard Jesus and have been taught by Him according to the truth that is in Him, then you know to take off your former way of life, your crumpled old self—that dark blot of a soul corrupted by deceitful desire and lust—to take a fresh breath and to let God renew your attitude and spirit.

Included in those choices is whether to obey the law. But that's a whole new page by itself!

Obeying the laws—all of them—not just a few—is a choice. God doesn't operate a cafeteria where you can just pick and choose which laws to obey. He makes that clear in Romans 13:1–5 (TLB).

> Obey the government, for God is the one who has put it there. There is no government anywhere that God has not placed in power. So those who refuse to obey the laws of the land are refusing to obey God, and punishment will follow. For the policeman does not frighten people who are doing right; but those doing evil will always fear him. So if you don't want to be afraid, keep the laws and you will get along well. The policeman is sent by God to help you. But if you are doing something wrong, of course you should be afraid, for he will have you punished. He is sent by God for that very purpose. Obey the laws then, for two reasons: first, to keep from being punished, and second, just because you know you should.

I see only two choices in this passage—either choose to obey all the laws or choose to break them. I don't see any bending of the law mentioned. Do you?

Tough choices are never easy—but the right choices will benefit you every time.

Wrong choices almost always seem the easiest at the time, but do they ever come back to haunt us! We've all made wrong choices. You are not alone. What you do with the consequences of that wrong choice will determine your future with God. Do you turn to Him or run away? Read what happens when you turn toward Him in Psalm 28:7 (KJV):

> The Lord is my strength and my shield; my heart trusted in
> him, and I am helped: therefore my heart greatly rejoiceth;
> and with my song will I praise him.

Notice the second *and* in that scripture. My heart trusts, and I am helped. What comes first—the help or the trust? God wants you to depend on Him and Him alone. Too often I try, on my own, to fix problems first, and if that doesn't work, then I turn to God. My fixes never work—they just delay the help.

Unwavering means *continuing in a strong and steady way, constant or steadfast.* Do you have constant trust in God? Neither do I, unfortunately—but I found someone in the Bible who had the same issue. Read about it in Mark 9:24 (KJV):

> And straightway the father of the child cried out, and said
> with tears, Lord, I believe; help thou mine unbelief.

This man was speaking to Jesus—he took his doubts to God. Why? Read on.

DAY 110

Maybe this father of a sick child had doubted numerous times that his child would be healed. He may have felt like the person mentioned in James 1:5–8 (KJV).

> If any of you lack wisdom let him ask of God, that giveth to all men liberally, and upbraideth not; and it shall be given him. But let him ask in faith, nothing wavering. For he that wavereth is like a wave of the sea driven with the wind and tossed. For let not that man think that he shall receive any thing of the Lord. A doubleminded man is unstable in all his ways.

Have you ever felt that you only make wrong choices? Could it be because you ask God but, in your heart, really doubt He will answer? I have. Perhaps this father had, and he was tired of it, so he went straight to the source. That verb *upbraideth*? It means *scold angrily*. God doesn't do that!

DAY 111

Why tell Jesus when you doubt? The answer lies in Hebrews 12:2 (NLV).

> Let us keep looking to Jesus. Our faith comes from Him
> and He is the One Who makes it perfect. He did not give up
> when He had to suffer shame and die on a cross. He knew
> of the joy that would be His later. Now He is sitting at the
> right side of God.

What a novel idea! Take your doubts to the one whom you are doubting. Why not give it a try?

Did you wonder who or what the words were when we quoted Mark 9:24? It's this same father pleading with Jesus after telling Him about his son's illness. Let's look at that in Mark 9:22b–23 (KJV):

> But if thou canst do any thing, have compassion on us, and
> help us. Jesus said unto him, If thou canst believe, all things
> are possible to him that believeth.

Obviously, this father believed in Jesus or he wouldn't have brought his son to Jesus to be healed. That's why he answered Jesus with the statement that he was a believer, but he still doubted. A wonderful example for us. When you doubt, go straight to the source. He is the one to whom we take our doubts and fears.

Call to me and I will answer you and tell you great
and unsearchable things you do not know.
Jeremiah 33:3 (NIV)

Day 112

We've talked about doubts, but what about fears? Sometimes they come on like a flood. Years ago when fear would try to overtake me, I had my little packet of verses that I would start quoting. Among them was Psalm 34:4: (KJV):

> I sought the Lord, and he heard me, and delivered me from
> all my fears.

But sometimes He didn't answer as quickly as I wanted, so I would go on to my next scripture, 2 Timothy 1:7 (KJV):

> For God hath not given us the spirit of fear; but of power,
> and of love, and of a sound mind.

There were times when I certainly didn't feel that I had a spirit of power! Have you ever felt paralyzed by fear? That good mind doesn't help a lot when it won't work. And love? Forget that. When you are paralyzed by fear, your only thought is survival.

And then a new day dawned, and I found that fighting fear is just that—a fight, and I needed some help—some power and some weapons. God has already provided the power and the weapons of warfare, and they are found in Ephesians 6:10–17 (NIV). Let's start gearing up!

DAY 113

Are you ready for a battle? First you must go through basic training! Most soldiers are highly trained in their fields, but all must start with the basics. Let's take Ephesians 6:10–17, bit by bit, beginning with Ephesians 6:10 (NIV):

> Finally, be strong in the Lord and in his mighty power.

Well, that's a great statement! Tell me to be strong, Lord! Right now I'm feeling mighty weak. I know You have mighty power, but how can I be strong in You? He never leaves us hanging—His answer is in the next verse. Read Ephesians 6:11 (NIV):

> Put on the full armor of God, so that you can take your
> stand against the devil's schemes.

In the military sense, to "take a stand" means holding your ground when you face the enemy. You don't let him invade your territory. To do that we must put on the full—not just partial—armor of God.

Remember that word—*stand*. It will occur several times as we look at the armor of God.

DAY 114

We don't want to shoot down our allies, so we must know who is the real enemy. Sometimes he comes at us disguised as someone or something else. Read Ephesians 6:12 (NIV).

> For our struggle is not against flesh and blood, but against the rulers, against the authorities, against the powers of this dark world and against the spiritual forces of evil in the heavenly realms.

Try always to assess your problems in the light of this verse. It may seem that people are harming us when, in reality, it's Satan himself.

After I felt God speaking to me to write this book, I put aside all other activities to devote my time to it. What happened? First our AC unit started leaking. A technician came out, found the problem, and fixed it. This created a small interruption but was no big deal—except that the AC still leaked. After six repair visits and eight technicians over a month, the problem was identified and repaired. By that time the leak had caused parts of the hardwood flooring to buckle. That called for another repair.

Then the light bulb went on—it was Satan trying to stop the book from being finished. It was such a futile effort that we had a good laugh, and I went back to work. I'm sure he will try again, but I'm onto him now and ready for battle. Why? Because of the armor of God.

Maybe someone has hurt you, and you feel resentment toward that person. Satan can use that bitterness in your heart to put a wedge between you and God. It's not the person who is the enemy. It's how you deal with Satan's plan to cause your defeat. Sure, the hurtful actions were wrong, but that's not the question. The question is, "How is your heart?" Focus on Ephesians 6:13 (NIV).

> Therefore put on the full armor of God, so that when the day of evil comes, you may be able to stand your ground, and after you have done everything, to stand.

Stand appears twice in this verse. The first usage means *to defend your ground*. This is the battle against Satan. Once you've put on the full armor of God, you are ready for battle. The best part comes next: "after you have done everything, to stand."

That first stand is action—it is battle. After the battle (after you have done everything), comes the next stand. This is the victory stance. It is the calm after the storm. It is you—yes, you—standing, calm, at peace with God, and confident of His power at work in you. Is this what you want in your life? Keep reading.

DAY 116

Shall we get dressed? Start with Ephesians 6:14 (NIV):

> Stand firm then, with the belt of truth buckled around your
> waist, with the breastplate of righteousness in place.

There's *stand* again. This is no army of weaklings! The first piece of defensive clothing is the belt of truth. The Roman soldiers had a heavy woven belt around their waists—their middles. What is the focus or middle of your life? What is truth? Read John 14:6 (KJV):

> Jesus saith unto him, I am the way, the truth, and the life:
> no man cometh unto the Father, but by me.

If Jesus is the truth and you have accepted Him as your personal Lord and Savior, then He should be the center of your life—that belt around your waist. But do you sometimes need some help in understanding? Jesus knew that and gave this promise in John 15:26 (KJV):

> But when the Comforter is come, whom I will send unto you
> from the Father, even the Spirit of truth, which proceedeth
> from the Father, he shall testify of me.

There's your second source of truth—which, of course, leads back to Jesus. Buckle that belt around your middle and get ready for the next piece.

The second half of Ephesians 6:14 is the "breastplate of righteousness." A breastplate is a piece of heavy bronze or other materials that covers and protects vital organs—like the heart.

Without a heart, we can't live, so this was a very important piece of the armor. But where do we get righteousness? I found the answer in 2 Corinthians 5:21 (AMP).

> He made Christ who knew no sin to (judicially) be sin on our behalf, so that in Him we would become the righteousness of God (that is, we would be made acceptable to Him and placed in a right relationship with Him by His gracious lovingkindness).

Jesus is also our righteousness! He paid the price for us to have it.

This breastplate was made with a buckle attached to the belt. If the belt isn't fastened tightly enough, the breastplate will fall off. That breastplate of righteousness only stays on with the belt of truth. Without Jesus, your whole body is vulnerable. First things first!

Take a good look, friends, at who you were when you got called into this life. I don't see many of "the brightest and the best" among you, not many influential, not many from high-society families. Isn't it obvious that God deliberately chose men and women that the culture overlooks and exploits and abuses, chose these "nobodies" to expose the hollow pretensions of the "somebodies"? That makes it quite clear that none of you can get by with blowing your own horn before God. Everything that we have—right thinking and right living, a clean slate and a fresh start—comes from God by way of Jesus Christ. That's why we have the saying, "If you're going to blow a horn, blow a trumpet for God."

1 Corinthians 1:26-31 (MSG)

DAY 118

Remember all those repetitions of the word *stand*? Now we are getting to what makes you stand firmly. Consider Ephesians 6:15 (NIV):

> And with your feet fitted with the readiness that comes from the gospel of peace.

A Roman soldier's sandals were heavy, multilayered leather shoes with spikes on the bottoms. Battles can be fought on slippery ground. To stand firmly, a soldier had to be ready at all times. Those spikes gave him traction to stand and not slip as the enemy approached. He could hold his ground.

Their shoes were a vital part of their equipment, just as the readiness that comes from the gospel of peace is vital to our spiritual battles. Where do we get that? We learn in 1 John 5:14–15 (KJV).

> And this is the confidence that we have in him, that, if we ask any thing according to his will, he heareth us: And if we know that he hear us, whatsoever we ask, we know that we have the petitions that we desired of him.

Confidence in our leader will give us peace. Having no doubts in Him makes us ready to stand firmly.

DAY 119

Read Ephesians 6:16 (NIV):

> In addition to all this, take up the shield of faith, with which
> you can extinguish all the flaming arrows of the evil one.

When we think of a shield these days, it's a small metal contraption held out and moved up and down or back and forth as needed. You'd better be quick to protect yourself from flaming arrows!

The Roman soldiers had a different type of shield. It was large enough to cover them from head to toe. When they put their shields up in front of them, they were fully protected. Remember that word *stand*? They could stand their ground with the shield in place.

So it's appropriate that the shield here is not made of wood or leather but of faith. What kind of arrows does the enemy shoot at you? Doubt? Condemnation? Fear?

With that shield of faith, you can stand your ground, confident in the God you serve to cover you with His protection. And what more could you need? Maybe you need more armor. That's for tomorrow.

DAY 120

You're almost ready for battle. This final verse, Ephesians 6:17 (NIV) tells how to finish arming yourself:

> Take the helmet of salvation and the sword of the Spirit, which is the word of God.

The helmet of salvation—what's that? It's the knowledge that you are a child of God. Remember when you accepted Jesus into your heart and were saved? It's now important that you keep that reality alive in your mind.

A helmet covers your head and protects your brain, where thoughts originate. Here's that issue of choice again. Keep that helmet buckled on, and every time the enemy comes at you with thoughts of doubt, fear, or condemnation, refuse them and remember Titus 3:3–8 (KJV).

> For we ourselves also were sometimes foolish, disobedient, deceived, serving divers lusts and pleasures, living in malice and envy, hateful, and hating one another. But after that the kindness and love of God our Saviour toward man appeared, Not by works of righteousness which we have done, but according to his mercy he saved us, by the washing of regeneration, and renewing of the Holy Ghost; Which he shed on us abundantly through Jesus Christ our Saviour; That being justified by his grace, we should be made heirs according to the hope of eternal life. This is a faithful saying, and these things I will that thou affirm constantly, that they which have believed in God might be careful to maintain good works. These things are good and profitable unto men.

Ephesians 6:17 (NIV) instructs us,

> Take the helmet of salvation and the sword of the Spirit,
> which is the word of God.

Notice that there is only one offensive item in this entire list of the armor of God. It's the sword of the Spirit, which is the Word of God.

You have all the protection you need, but when the enemy keeps coming, get tough! Use that sword.

The Bible also describes the Word of God as a sword in Hebrews 4:12 (KJV).

> For the word of God is quick, and powerful, and sharper
> than any twoedged sword, piercing even to the dividing
> asunder of soul and spirit and of the joint and marrow, and
> is a discerner of the thoughts and intents of the heart. .

What soldier would go to battle with a dull sword? No soldier would. He would keep his weapon sharp. So must you also—you never know when the enemy could appear.

You sharpen your sword, the Word of God, by spending time every day reading and meditating on His word. Have you sharpened your sword today?

DAY 122

Since God is so interested in keeping our bodies safe from the enemy, should we also be concerned about them? Read 1 Corinthians 6:19–20 (KJV):

> What? know ye not that your body is the temple of the Holy Ghost which is in you, which ye have of God, and ye are not your own?

Honor God with my body? How do I do that? Saint Paul wrote here about how we treat ourselves. Here we go back again to those choices. Read 1 Corinthians 6:12–13 (TLB).

> I can do anything I want to if Christ has not said no, but some of these things aren't good for me. Even if I am allowed to do them, I'll refuse to if I think they might get such a grip on me that I can't easily stop when I want to. For instance, take the matter of eating. God has given us an appetite for food and stomachs to digest it. But that doesn't mean we should eat more than we need.

Are you putting food or substances that are not good for you into your body?

DAY 123

What you put into your body through your mouth, nose, and veins is important, but there's more. Let's go back and get the full meaning of yesterday's scripture in 1 Corinthians by backing up two verses to 1 Corinthians 6:17–20 (TLB).

> But if you give yourself to the Lord, you and Christ are joined together as one person. That is why I say to run from sex sin. No other sin affects the body as this one does. When you sin this sin it is against your own body. Haven't you yet learned that your body is the home of the Holy Spirit God gave you, and that he lives within you? Your own body does not belong to you. For God has bought you with a great price. So use every part of your body to give glory back to God because he owns it.

When discussing how we treat our bodies, sometimes it sounds like a big *no* sermon, but the Bible is full of examples of the blessings people received when they followed God's instructions. Read Proverbs 10:30 (TLB):

> The good shall never lose God's blessings, but the wicked shall lose everything.

Are you ready for more of God's blessings? Let's keep going!

Day 124

Read Proverbs 17:22 (NASB):

> A happy heart is good medicine and a joyful mind causes
> healing, But a broken spirit dries up the bones.

One of the greatest blessings from God is joy, but this verse takes joy one step further in stating that a happy mind causes healing. The medical community has now discovered the value of a patient's frame of mind in healing.

Notice "a happy heart is good medicine." Most of us take medicine from time to time. Sometimes it works, and sometimes it doesn't. Researchers are always searching for effective drugs that work every time on everybody.

Is your heart happy? Read Proverbs 15:13 (NIV):

> A happy heart makes the face cheerful, but heartache
> crushes the spirit.

Do you have a clown face? A smile that is painted on but doesn't come from the heart? Those are the hardest ones.

Did you notice that both verses list the good outcomes (happiness and joy) first, and the bad outcomes (broken or crushed spirits) second? That's because it takes the good medicine to heal your spirit. So where do we get this drug? You guessed it—that's for tomorrow.

DAY 125

Do you feel crushed in spirit? Has someone or something hurt you so much that you feel unworthy to live? Or maybe bad choices on your part put you where you are, and there seems no way out.

Don't listen to all those negative thoughts! Look up—there's a way out. Wipe off that painted-on smile and see what can happen in your life in Psalm 30:1–3 (MSG).

> I give you all the credit, God—you got me out of that mess, you didn't let my foes gloat. God, my God, I yelled for help and you put me together. God, you pulled me out of the grave, gave me another chance at life when I was down-and-out.

What was David's first action? He yelled for help; he prayed. It's okay to tell God everything. Pour it all out to Him. And then what happened? Let's read the next two verses.

> All you saints! Sing your hearts out to God! Thank him to his face! He gets angry once in a while, but across a lifetime there is only love. The nights of crying your eyes out give way to days of laughter. (Psalm 30:4–5 MSG)

Day 126

Days of laughter? That's a lot of genuine smiles! Would you have a happy heart if you could be taken out of your present situation? Most of us would. But altering life's circumstances won't change a crushed spirit. That takes much healing. You can find it right where you are—no matter where that is. Read what Jesus said on this topic in Luke 4:18a (KJV):

> The Spirit of the Lord is upon me, because he hath anointed me to preach the gospel to the poor; he hath sent me to heal the brokenhearted.

You can go to Jesus anytime, anywhere, and get the healing you need.

There are times when healing takes longer than we would wish. Just as the sun won't rise at midnight when we want, God's healing of your broken spirit may take longer. Trust Him and don't doubt just because it doesn't happen instantaneously.

Go back to the beginning of your first time with Him. Did you pour out all your feelings? Or did you keep some of them back because you thought He wouldn't approve? He wants your total and complete trust in Him. Give it and watch for that sunrise!

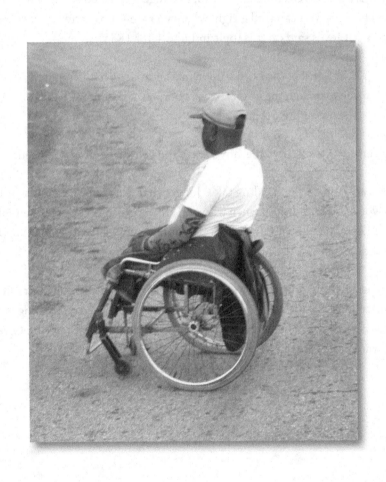

Day 127

We're back to the joyful mind that causes healing.

Do you have a happy heart that is evidenced by a genuine smile? Maybe it's time to count your blessings. Is your list short? I don't think so—start with the fact that you have air to breathe. Compare your life with someone else's. Focus on your blessings instead of the misfortunes.

Have you read God's Word today? If you've accepted Jesus into your heart, you have eternal life after this one. Is that something you can find joy in?

Joy and peace are often joined together for good reason. The true joy of the Lord brings peace.

Study Romans 15:13 (KJV):

> Now the God of hope fill you with all joy and peace in believing, that ye may abound in hope, through the power of the Holy Ghost.

What else will joy do for you?

DAY 128

Joy isn't given just so you can feel good. It comes to you because of Jesus. Read 1 Peter 1:8–9 (VOICE).

> Although you haven't seen Jesus, you still love Him. Although you don't yet see Him, you do believe in Him and celebrate with a joy that is glorious and beyond words. You are receiving the salvation of your souls as the result of your faith.

If that isn't enough, there's more! Consider Nehemiah 8:10 (MSG).

> He continued, "Go home and prepare a feast, holiday food and drink; and share it with those who don't have anything; This day is holy to God. Don't feel bad. The joy of God is your strength!"

So joy gives you strength. But if you have joy, why do you need strength? Don't think for a minute that the enemy is not going to try to rob you of your joy. Remember the battle and the armor? God's promises will fill your mind with confidence. Let's look at them.

Day 129

Here's a promise to repeat to yourself every day. Read it in Deuteronomy 31:8 (NIV):

> The Lord himself goes before you and will be with you; he will never leave you nor forsake you. Do not be afraid; do not be discouraged.

The dictionary defines *never* as *at no time in the past or future; on no occasion; not ever.* It defines *forsake* as *abandon.* So look at this promise: The Lord will not ever, at any time in the future, or on any occasion, leave you or abandon you.

That means that, whether or not you feel His presence, He is there with you. That's a promise you can hold onto. We took several days with Psalm 23. Let's look again at verse 6a (NIV): "Surely your goodness and love will follow me all the days of my life."

If the Lord himself goes before you, and His goodness and love follow you, you're surrounded by His protection! That's why He tells us over and over to not be afraid.

But we're just getting started with His promises.

DAY 130

Let's look at more promises that God will never leave you or abandon you. Isaiah 49:16a (TLB) goes further:

> See, I have tattooed your name upon my palm.

How's that for a permanent reminder of who you are to Him? It boggles my imagination that God can love me that much, but His word is truth, so I can believe it.

Here's another verse that shows Jesus has a permanent record of all His children. It's found in Revelation 3:5 (AMP).

> He who overcomes (the world through believing that Jesus is the Son of God) will accordingly be dressed in white clothing; and I will never blot out his name from the Book of Life, and I will confess and openly acknowledge his name before My Father and before His angels (saying that he is one of Mine).

Here is Jesus talking about you and me—in white clothing, no less—which indicates how completely he has cleansed us from all past sins. He, Jesus, is telling His Father God our names from His Book of Life, (eternal) and the Father has tattooed your name and mine on His hand. There is no way you will ever be forgotten again!

DAY 131

Read these words in Isaiah 54:10 (KJV).

> For the mountains shall depart, and the hills be removed; but my kindness shall not depart from thee, neither shall the covenant of my peace be removed, saith the Lord that hath mercy on thee.

How's that for an assurance of peace in your life? Is it always there? Not necessarily—if we try to act in our ways instead of God's way. Consider Proverbs 3:5–6 (KJV):

> Trust in the Lord with all thine heart; and lean not unto thine own understanding. In all thy ways acknowledge him, and he shall direct thy paths.

This takes time—listening time. When you face a decision, take a time-out—not to stand in the corner but to listen. Instead of roaring ahead with your plans, let your loving heavenly Father give you insight. Then the peace of God will overtake you.

DAY 132

Do you like waiting? I certainly don't! That is, until I found this verse in Isaiah 40:31 (KJV):

> But they that wait upon the Lord shall renew their strength;
> they shall mount up with wings as eagles; they shall run,
> and not be weary; and they shall walk and not faint.

This makes waiting sound worthwhile. I will get renewed strength? If you've ever watched an eagle in the sky, its flight looks so effortless. Have you wished your life could be that easy? Perhaps it could get simpler if we knew God's plan. That plan is the topic in Jeremiah 29:11 (AMP):

> For I know the plans and thoughts that I have for you,'"
> says the Lord, "'plans for peace and well-being and not for
> disaster, to give you a future and a hope.

There's *peace* again. God's plan is for peace. So how do I find out what his plan is for me? Try listening after you ask Him. That takes time. A quick prayer asking Him to bless your plans won't do. Give Him some of your time, wait, and see what happens!

Do you think maybe God got you mixed up with someone else and gave you His plan for that other person? Do you ask, "Why is all this happening to me?" Try 2 Corinthians 1:3–4 (KJV).

> Blessed be God, even the Father of our Lord Jesus Christ, the Father of mercies, and the God of all comfort; Who comforteth us in all our tribulation, that we may be able to comfort them which are in any trouble, by the comfort wherewith we ourselves are comforted of God.

Is there a purpose for your problems—those that you didn't create? Could it be part of God's plan? Remember that God deals in eternal issues—He has your whole life's plan in front of Him. We see only a bit of it at a time. That's why we can rest, as we are advised in Romans 8:28 (KJV):

> And we know that all things work together for good to them that love God, to them who are the called according to his purpose.

Day 134

Okay, so now I know that God has a plan—a unique plan—for my life. But there are times when my life just doesn't look like a plan. It looks more like chaos. Does that mean that I have messed up? First things first. Run—don't walk—to Him. Why? Read Psalm 34:17 (KJV):

> The righteous cry, and the Lord heareth, and delivereth them out of all their troubles.

Here's your rescue plan. Go to God with all your troubles. Obviously He knew you would have them because He provided the answer before you needed it.

Let's backtrack to the issue of messing up. Maybe you did—it probably wasn't your first time, and it won't be the last, but the answer is always the same, as found in 1 John 1:9 (KJV):

> If we confess our sins, he is faithful and just to forgive us our sins, and to cleanse us from all unrighteousness.

There is another of His wonderful promises! So relax and lean back on His loving kindness while we look at more promises.

Day 135

Once you have lived as long as I have, you can look back and see how God's plan for your life has worked. Hindsight is always easy. Now I can see why I had to wait on that answer to the prayer I prayed for ten years. But I still need help with decisions and directions—I don't want to get off God's plan at this late date! Here's a verse I cling to—James 1:5 (AMP).

> If any of you lacks wisdom (to guide him through a decision or circumstance), he is to ask of (our benevolent) God, who gives to everyone generously and without rebuke or blame, and it will be given to him.

When I was about twelve, I heard about a man in the Bible who pleased God. Wow! Could I be like that man? What did he do? He asked God for wisdom. It was Solomon after he had been made king. God appeared to him in a dream and told him to ask for anything he wanted. Now that's a dream. How would you answer that question? Solomon asked for wisdom. Read what happened in 1 Kings 3:10 (TLB):

> The Lord was pleased with his reply and was glad that Solomon had asked for wisdom.

Do you want to please God? Ask for wisdom!

DAY 136

The Bible is full of reassurances for us. Over and over again, God tells us to not be afraid. Why did he do that? Could it be because there are constantly people or events that bring a new kind of fear? But fear is fear. Here is a scripture to memorize so that you are prepared when a new fear hits you.

> 'Do not fear (anything), for I am with you; do not be afraid, for I am your God. I will strengthen you, be assured I will help you; I will certainly take hold of you with My righteous right hand (a hand of justice, of power, of victory, of salvation).' (Isaiah 41:10 AMP)

What a promise! And because He wants to be sure you heard Him, He repeats Himself in Isaiah 41:13 (AMP):

> For I the Lord your God keep hold of your right hand; (I am the Lord), Who says to you, 'Do not fear, I will help you.

Memorize these verses, underline them here, dog-ear the page, put a marker at this site—do whatever it takes to remember that the God of the universe is right beside you!

DAY 137

Have you received your invitation from Jesus to His party? It may have been lost in the mail. If so, here is a copy of it in Mark 2:17 (MSG):

> Jesus, overhearing, shot back, 'Who needs a doctor: the healthy or the sick? I'm here inviting the sin-sick, not the spiritually-fit.

Here is practical info about this invitation. Jesus does not host costume parties. He doesn't ask you to dress up and pretend you're someone else. His invitations are always "come as you are."

> Come on now, let's walk and talk; let's work this out. Your wrongdoings are bloodred, but they can turn as white as snow. Your sins are red like crimson, but they can be made clean again like new wool. (Isaiah 1:18 VOICE)

He invites you to bring all your junk, your past, and all those mistakes and wrong choices to this party for two. No need to dress up and pretend to be what you want others to think you are. Jesus has open arms—will you accept His invitation?

RSVP

If you have accepted Jesus's invitation, make a record of it here for all to see. Be proud of your newfound faith and friend!

I accepted Jesus as my personal Lord and Savior and have made Him Lord of my life.

Name:

_____

Date:

_____

The purpose of this book has been to share the love of Jesus with you. Would you go to our website and tell us about your experience? Find us at http://www.yourinvitationbook.com.

We would love to chat with you. Contact us via our blog on the above website. May God continue to bless you richly in your daily walk with Him.

Comments on the KJV

We have used several versions of the Bible when quoting scripture. Some of the more modern versions make the meaning clearer since they are in today's language.

The standard on which most Bibles are based is the King James Version, and we have quoted from it in many places. Don't let the *thees* and *thous* throw you. To understand more about this version, we need to look at how it came to be.

In 1604 King James saw the need for a Bible that could be read to everyone in churches and that everyone could understand. He appointed about fifty of England's finest language scholars to complete the task. They were told to use old, familiar terms and names and make the work readable in the idioms of the day. An idiom is figurative language like "It's raining cats and dogs." We all know that doesn't mean kittens and puppies are falling from the sky but that we are receiving a heavy rain. However, the idioms of the 1600s are not the ones we have today. That doesn't mean the KJV is not accurate—just that its usages are different from the ways we speak today.

The other main difference is in some pronouns used in that day. They used *ye* for *you* plural, *thee* and *thou* rather than our singular *you*, and *thy* and *thine* for *your* or *yours*. They also added many *-est* and *-th* ending to words.

If yours is a KJV Bible, try this little experiment when reading it to see if it helps your understanding. Here's Matthew 6:17–18 (KJV).

> But thou, when thou fastest, anoint thine head, and wash thy face. That thou appear not unto men to fast, but unto thy Father which is in secret; and thy Father, which seeth in secret, shall reward thee openly.

Now try reading it as I do.

> But you, when you fast, anoint your head, and wash your
> face. That you appear not unto men to fast, but unto your
> Father which is in secret; and your Father, which sees in
> secret, shall reward you openly.

We didn't change the meaning at all!

A few other points to note about the KJV: Some terms, like *man*, refer not only to males but to mankind—the human race. Words can change meaning over the years. For instance, the KJV uses *Holy Ghost* to refer to the third person of the Trinity. We now refer to Him as the Holy Spirit. Instead of *verily*, we say *truly*. We say *different* instead of *divers* and *worry* instead of *fret*. A good Bible dictionary can help you with terms that seem different to you.

Try reading without the *thees* and *thous* and the old-style endings to some words when you find the KJV quoted in the pages here. You'll find that it sounds more like what God would say today. We serve a God who speaks every language and uses the idioms of our day. Just listen!

The thief cometh not, but for to steal, and to kill, and
to destroy: I am come that they might have life, and
that they might have it more abundantly.
John 10:10 (KJV)

Printed in the United States
By Bookmasters